# GARDENING
# WITH BULBS

# GARDENING WITH BULBS

## A PRACTICAL GUIDE

Cathy Buchanan

THE NATIONAL TRUST

Published in Great Britain in 1999
The National Trust (Enterprises) Ltd
36 Queen Anne's Gate
London SW1H 9AS

ISBN 0 7078 0320 9

Cataloguing in Publication Data is available from the
British Library

All photographs are from the National Trust Photographic
Library and are by the following photographers:
Stephen Robson: front cover, frontispiece, pp.6, 22, 23, 27, 31,
39, 43, 47, 50-1, 59, 62, 63, 66, 74, 78, 83, 86, back cover
Ray Hallett: p.11
Nick Meers: pp.15, 35
Neil Campbell-Sharp: p.71

Line drawings by Jim Robins

Designed and typeset in Palatino by the
Newton Engert Partnership

Production by Louise Pope

Printed in Great Britain by Butler & Tanner Limited

FRONTISPIECE: *Lilium martagon* var. *cattaniae* is a fine,
easily grown, vigorous lily which tolerates sun or partial
shade and thrives even in the damp climate of the
Lily Wood at Mount Stewart.

# Contents

# Introduction

A visit to a National Trust garden in spring to see sheets of crocus, fritillaries and narcissus extending hundreds of yards is like visiting a national art gallery. Just to know that this glory exists somewhere and is given the conditions of love and cultural attention it deserves is for many of us deeply satisfying, but gardeners will always be inspired to recreate some of this magic at home. Although the ten talented Head Gardeners who contributed to this book will testify to the importance of their horticultural manipulation of these rivers and trickles of colour, all would also vouch for the role of chance and vision in gardening with bulbs.

At best it is never a struggle against nature, but governed by those things that the soil and the garden seem to demand. Continual observation is crucial, as is an understanding of the natural habitat in which a wild bulb thrives. Experiences of failure have been as vital to the Head Gardeners' deep fund of knowledge as the successes visitors enjoy each year. And, although you might argue that the odd 'off' year when narcissus fly has struck and the daffodil display much reduced is of less consequence for a twenty-five acre garden than for a modest plot, it is still heartening to hear the overall optimistic advice that gardeners should focus less on the problems and more on the joys of gardening with bulbs. In this book you will find plenty of successfully broken rules and few worries about the 'art' of gardening. These professionals, it seems, are not keen to give us a list of jobs for the week!

Another frequently voiced concern was that gardeners should be inspired by – rather than simply copy – the effects achieved in these magnificent gardens. As Sarah Cook at Sissinghurst said, 'Gardening is not just about seeing a plant association and then doing it at home. Really creative gardening is about growing plants in different ways, daring to grow certain bulbs in the sometimes harsh conditions they experience naturally, so that the plants are true to their own character. You must be continually learning from your garden what really makes your own plants tick. Good books are quite helpful, but they are just a starting point.'

This book is, hopefully, just such a starting point for the keen bulb grower. There is so much more to learn. Botany and an understanding of natural habitat creep endlessly into the subject of bulb-growing and it is noticeable that the Head Gardeners are generally more interested in habitat creation than in the details of planting bulbs at exactly the right depth. In other words, their primary concern is to ensure that the herbaceous plants and trees above a particular colony of bulbs

The old daffodil cultivars in the Wall Garden at Nymans are lifted and divided whenever flowering shows signs of tailing off due to the congestion of the clumps of bulbs.

provide just the right environment of shade, daylight and rainfall during the bulb's varying cycles of growth. The light shade cast by one particular tree or herbaceous plant (or even simply grass) may be just right for success, while the much heavier shade of different species would result in failure.

This is particularly noticeable in the discussions on snowdrops at Anglesey Abbey and woodland bulbs at Knightshayes, but applies to all of the bulbs in the book to a greater or lesser extent. While it is always advisable to plant a bulb at its correct depth, this may not be the most critical factor for success. Some bulbs have an inbuilt mechanism for pulling themselves to their ideal soil level – Richard Ayres' snowdrops growing happily on the compost heap where they were accidentally flung at Anglesey Abbey are a perfect illustration.

Anyone interested in growing bulbs is therefore well-advised by the Head Gardeners to understand that these are most usually wild plants and, as such, biologically adapted to a particular habitat, even though we grow them in our gardens. The main exceptions to this are the great hordes of daffodil, tulip or hyacinth cultivars which have been carefully cultivated and hybridised by man for centuries. Whenever you see a name such as *Narcissus* 'King Alfred', you should be immediately alerted by the so-called 'cultivar' name ('King Alfred' in this case) to the fact that it is likely to be a garden-bred form of the bulb, rather than a true wild plant. In exactly the same way, the domestic cat is related to the tiger.

This is as important practically as it is botanically. A big yellow trumpet daffodil such as 'King Alfred' is very well adapted over centuries of breeding to what we might call 'average' garden conditions and therefore relatively easy to grow. A wild narcissus species on the other hand, such as little *Narcissus bulbocodium*, is a far greater challenge in cultivation, as even in your garden it will still insist on conditions which approximate to those experienced in the wild.

The example above raises another tricky question, namely our over-reliance on common names. If you like daffodils and want only to grow the big cheerful trumpets found in every garden centre, then by all means carry on calling them 'daffodils'. You will find them easy to please. If you want to be more adventurous and to expand your knowledge of this fascinating group, perhaps growing some of the daintiest tiny species of *Narcissus* which flower on rocky, barren soil only feet from mountain snow high up in the Pyrenees, then you had better learn to call these plants by their correct botanical name.

They are all, botanically-speaking, *Narcissus*, from the wild British 'Lent lily' or 'daffodil', *N. pseudonarcissus*, to the white Poet's 'narcissus', *Narcissus poeticus*. Learning this botanical language opens up whole new areas of understanding. Not only can you glean more from the best gardening books, but you can also talk confidently to gardening friends in the sure knowledge that you are both discussing the same plant.

While I talked with each gardener, from Nigel Marshall at Mount Stewart in Northern Ireland to Michael Hickson at Knightshayes in Devon, we wandered continually over the hazy botanical boundaries of the 'true' bulbs into the grey area of related plants which produce similar tough underground storage organs to help them endure extreme conditions – usually of drought – in their native habitat. To understand the mechanism, you only have to think of a deciduous tree which loses its leaves in the cold northern winter. It goes dormant in order to survive, in just the same way as do the bulbs.

But where does one draw the boundaries? It is useful to know that botanists classify them according to the parts of the plant from which each has evolved. True 'bulbs' (such as many members of the lily family including lily, tulip, fritillary) are modified underground shoots, made up of fleshy, colourless leaves or leaf bases wrapped around a bud, and these organs persist in the ground for more than one season. Corms (as in many members of the iris family, including crocus and crocosmia) are compact, swollen underground stems without the fleshy leaves, and usually each individual corm withers and dies at the end of the season, having meanwhile produced a replacement corm. Tubers (like cyclamen or arum) are solid, modified underground stems or roots. Those evolved from a stem (such as potato) may be distinguished from root tubers (like dahlias) by the presence of buds or 'eyes' on the tuber. Rhizomes (as in some iris) are the final main class of underground storage organ. These are a form of modified, horizontal stem.

Many tubers and rhizomes (which are less obviously bulb-like in appearance) will be found rubbing shoulders with the 'true' bulbs and corms in the bulb retailer's catalogue. The space available in a short book dictates, however, that at least a few lines must be drawn. The bulk of the practical information is therefore focused on the 'true' bulbs of tulip, daffodil, lily, hyacinth, snowdrop and fritillary, as well as the corms of crocus. However, where the Head Gardener's passion for a particular plant has led us into the realms of the fragile little rhizomatous woodland anemones or the wonderful 'dinner plate' tubers of a mature cyclamen, the temptation to follow is impossible to resist.

# Anglesey Abbey

CAMBRIDGESHIRE

Area: 40ha (98 acres)
Soil: Good, medium loam on
   clay base. Neutral to slightly
   alkaline
Altitude: 0·6m (2ft)
Average rainfall: 533mm (21in)
Average climate: Continental,
   with very cold winters and
   hot, dry summers

Dazzling light and dark shadow leave a powerful image of Anglesey Abbey imprinted on the visitor's memory. These elements are repeatedly used – like an artist's brush strokes – to create drama and mood: brilliant sunshine over a shimmering lawn and long meadow grass is juxtaposed with the cool, leafy cover of broad avenues; exuberant dahlias are only a few feet from a narrow, shady path where snowdrops shelter, sleeping away the summer's heat.

Huttleston Broughton, later 1st Lord Fairhaven, was tempted to Anglesey Abbey in 1926 by the alluring combination of good racing and excellent shooting right on his doorstep. It seems, however, that he soon caught gardening fever, spurred on by his natural love of trees. Beyond the intimate embrace of the small Victorian garden that surrounded the house – constructed around the ruins of an Augustinian Priory – he began to realise his vision of a grand twentieth-century landscape garden on the flat, featureless Cambridgeshire fens.

Armed with planting advice from landscape architect Lanning Roper and Newmarket neighbour, Major Vernon Daniell, he walked the grounds with his Head Gardener, Noel Ayres, bamboo canes in hand, placing them here or there to mark the breadth and stretch of each planned walk or the perfect position for so many precious trees. In this way a remarkable tracery of allées, walks, vistas, arboreta and formal gardens grew, which he punctuated with historical garden statuary, in keeping with the grand style of the garden he created.

RICHARD AYRES is the second in a succession of Ayres to lead the five-man gardening team at Anglesey Abbey. As the son of the 1st Lord Fairhaven's Head Gardener, Noel Ayres, he began gardening himself at Anglesey in 1959 and finally took over from his father in 1973. Although never formally trained, his practical apprenticeship must have begun as soon as he could walk and his understanding of the garden, with all its eccentricities in cultivation, is profound. Richard remembers how Lord Fairhaven used to survey the grounds with his father, planning and planting – and no doubt arguing amicably. 'I like to think that Lord Fairhaven left us the bones of a great garden to which we are now adding the flesh,' he reflects.

## Bulbs at Anglesey Abbey

Lord Fairhaven was a great advocate of what Richard calls 'splash' gardening, with everything geared to a seasonal peak

The serried ranks of thousands of blue and white hyacinths are the first breath-taking sight to greet the visitor when Anglesey Abbey opens to the public each March.

of perfection in different areas of the garden. In June and July the Herbaceous Garden had reliably to stop his guests in their tracks, while later in the season the Dahlia Garden was the highlight of a stroll round the grounds. Naturally, bulbs were an important element in the 'splash' technique. Hence the wondrous, if desperately brief, vision of the Hyacinth Garden during late March – four thousand perfectly regular blooms of blue and white standing to attention like soldiers, at the precise moment visitors are welcomed back for the season.

'Everything we do at Anglesey must be big,' Richard smiles. 'We can't have small patches of snowdrops, narcissus or fritillaries here and I imagine great sheets of them for the future!' One plan involves planting *Fritillaria meleagris* in the damp, open area called The Squares. To achieve the vast drifts of snakeshead fritillary, he determines to plant 5,000 bulbs a year: 'I kid the other gardeners that we are going to keep going until we reach the road!'

## The Snowdrops

One of the garden's best known features of recent years – the phenomenal display of snowdrops – owes much to Richard's own passion. It all started with Anglesey's most famous snowdrop, *Galanthus lagodechianus*, which he discovered on a rubbish tip that serviced the Victorian garden in the early 1960s.

'There had always been a few snowdrops about in that area', Richard recalls, 'but no one had really taken much notice of them until one February when I was working in the area and suddenly became aware that one type had particularly beautiful, bright green leaves.'

After expert identification, the gardeners realised that they had a very rare species from the Caucasus on their hands – possibly a relic of plantings one hundred years ago after the Crimean War. Over the next five years, five more distinctive forms were found in the same area and Richard began to bring them into the rest of the garden to encourage their spread.

There were already many naturalised double and single forms of the common snowdrop, *G. nivalis*, at Anglesey. However the identification of that rare species was the beginning of serious snowdrop collecting and led eventually to the annual 'Snowdrop Weekends', when the garden is specially opened to the public for two weekends in February. Now Richard confesses to a terminal case of 'galanthophilia' – from the botanical name for snowdrop, *Galanthus*!

'I'm sure that after I've retired, visitors will still find me on my zimmerframe crawling up between the banks of the Dell where the monks made their ponds before the fens were drained. Little did they realise what a perfect home this would be for our precious snowdrops.'

## Ideal Snowdrop Conditions

In their natural habitat, from Europe to Western Asia, most snowdrop species will receive plenty of moisture through an overhead canopy of leafless trees or shrubs in winter, while in the summer they benefit from the drier soil and shading. Richard finds the best snowdrop areas are characterised by dappled, slightly moist shade. At Anglesey, snowdrops grow best under the following conditions:

● *Sparse woodland plantings with enough light penetration for cow parsley and other wild flowers to thrive.* The Victorian rubbish dump is typical: grass is almost non-existent, but the wildflower undergrowth can be surprisingly rank in summer.

Snowdrops and winter aconite flourish even with rampant ivy, however management of the tree cover to maintain what Richard terms a 'parkland shade' must be precise: removing too much encourages coarse plants like nettles with which snowdrops cannot compete, but a little careful culling of the older trees and vigorous shrubs such as snowberry allows the snowdrops to really take off.

● *Open parkland and lawn areas where the ground cover of grass or other plants is thin due to mowing and the shade of large specimen trees.* Anglesey's largest drifts of naturalised snowdrops grow in areas like this. Richard says, 'You have to choose strong forms such as *G. nivalis* 'Flore Pleno' for these areas, as snowdrops don't really like competition from thick grass. Some gardeners spray off the grass with herbicide when the snowdrops are dormant, but I don't really like the visual effect of bare patches of earth.'

● *Areas with tree and shrub canopy but little competition from grasses and wildflowers.* The plantings on the mounds around the old monastic fishponds are typical. Originally these were covered by a canopy of sycamore and very old thorns, with a little ash or chestnut. Since the banks were colonised with snowdrops, philadelphus have been added as an understorey planting to the trees.

Each of these areas are strimmed in June, although a rotary mower may be used on the largest areas. The grass is raked off and removed. They will be strimmed or mown again at the very least in September, and the cuttings left to decay *in situ*, but grass where small spring wildflowers are naturalised is cut more regularly every six to eight weeks. Just before Christmas an effort is made to clear leaf debris so that the snowdrops are in full view come February.

## Cultivating Snowdrops

● Always plant snowdrops 'in the green' (i.e. in full growth) during February/March. This is when the best snowdrop suppliers offer bulbs for sale. The method is the same whether you transplant or are planting new bulbs.

● Richard feels that snowdrops are used to best effect in positions which become invisible during the summer months. 'Plant them in shrubberies where you can enjoy them early in the season, and where, when you start actively gardening your plot later, they will be easily forgotten and left in peace.'

● Lifting and dividing clumps is the best way to increase your snowdrops. Left alone they will thrive, but usually remain in small groups rather than creating a drift.

OPPOSITE: Snowdrops under trees at Anglesey Abbey. Once they have died down, snowdrops appreciate the slightly drying effect of the light summer shade.

● Bulbs can be moved in full flower. At Anglesey this is the best time for transplanting, because you can see which form you are dealing with, but they will never be out of the ground for more than half an hour. Richard says that dried bulbs planted in autumn rarely establish well, but those in full flower show little sign of disturbance after only a fortnight.

● Lift and divide the bulbs into groups of three to six so that they will bulk up into good sized clumps quickly. If you have the patience – or are dealing with a particularly expensive named cultivar – you can replant bulbs individually, but they will take longer to create a drift effect. Richard expects each mother bulb to produce an 'offset' or young bulb during its second season after planting, and thereafter to double up each year. In time, many will begin to self-sow.

● Snowdrops require the minimum of planting fuss if moved at the correct time, but if you think about the overall effect you are aiming for, you can create drifts that appear to have just happened. Richard plans his by eye, filling in the shape by planting clumps of three or four bulbs over the whole area.

● Lay the groups of bulbs on the surface of your drift, about 30cm (12in) apart (**a**). To plant, make a slit with a spade, handle the snowdrops by their foliage (**b**) and set them into the soil, firming hard with your heel against the slit (**c**).

Planting snowdrops in full growth or 'in the green'.

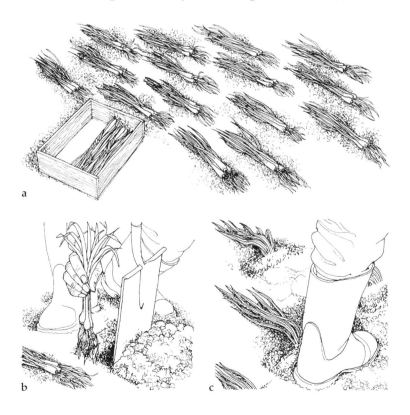

● Richard finds different snowdrops need different planting depths, because the size of the bulb varies. *G. elwesii* is usually planted about 5–7.5cm (2–3in) below soil level, whereas smaller *G. nivalis* 'Flore Pleno', is covered with only 2.5cm (1in) of soil. 'On the other hand, bulbs left lying on the surface of the rubbish tip seem to root and flower, then pull themselves down to their correct soil depth – which proves we needn't fret too much about mathematical precision!'

● If you plant snowdrops in areas which receive an annual mulch, Richard believes it is best to mulch after they have finished flowering, rather than in the autumn or when the bulbs are pushing through, as a thick mulch may distort the foliage as it emerges. Mulching after flowering can help deter narcissus fly which may enter snowdrop bulbs through the hole where the flowering stem emerged.

● Grey mould (*Botrytis cinerea*) is caused either by climate – over which you have no control – or by overcrowding; the best remedy is to lift and divide the clumps so that the bulbs are more widely spaced.

### Snowdrop Variation

The garden benefits regularly from the chance finds and swapping of treasures among 'galanthophiles' like Richard. 'Best of all, snowdrops show so much natural variation that there is really no need to hybridise or breed them. Some experts will remove the seedheads to prevent their promiscuous habits, but I prefer to let them do their own thing.'

Identification is hotly debated by enthusiasts, which is where addiction sets in: the longer you gaze the more bewitching every detail becomes. Each species has a distinctive leaf colour and formation, and many named snowdrops have a characteristic droop of flower. Often the colour and shape of the markings on the inner ring of 'tepals', the botanic term for the petals, is the best method of recognition.

### Recommended snowdrops for naturalising

*G. nivalis* **'Flore Pleno'** Narrow grey-green leaves. Richard finds that the double forms of the common snowdrop, *G. nivalis*, show up best in the distance as the classic drift of white we expect. They are also vigorous enough to compete with light grass.

*G. elwesii* Broad grey-green leaves, hooded at tips. A very variable snowdrop and one of the tallest, growing to over 25cm (10in) in some named forms. 'It actually looks like a cultivar, and is almost too big and bold to be a snowdrop,' comments Richard.

*Galanthus nivalis* 'Flore Pleno'

*Galanthus* 'Galatea'

*G. plicatus* Broad grey-green leaves, with edges 'plicate' or turned under. A big, grand snowdrop. 'Augustus' is a fine named *G. plicatus* hybrid and very vigorous, with green leaves covered in a beautiful grey bloom. Less suited to naturalising *en masse* are sweetly scented 'S. Arnott' and 'Magnet', with its fascinating, pronounced droop to the flowers. Both are probably a cross between *G. plicatus* and *G. elwesii*.

*G.* 'Galatea' Grey-green leaves. A strong-growing snowdrop, reminiscent of a 'Magnet' form in markings and habit, but earlier, larger, and unfortunately without the scent.

*G.* 'Merlin' Wide grey leaves. Related to *G. caucasicus*. Richard says, 'There's a good deal of disagreement about what constitutes a true 'Merlin'. The defining feature is said to be a heavy green stripe down the middle of the inner tepals. The form I prefer is questionably 'Merlin', but it droops so beautifully that it will definitely represent 'Merlin' in my own garden.'

### Four special Anglesey snowdrops

From the ninety-eight forms which have naturally arisen at Anglesey, a small selection of 'classics' are gradually being introduced to the public by commercial growers.

**'Richard Ayres'** Named for Richard, this is the largest double snowdrop he has seen, with a sweet scent as a bonus.

**'Alwyn'** Named for the 3rd Lord Fairhaven and also a double, Richard believes this is the most perfectly symmetrical snowdrop ever seen at Anglesey, but is unfortunately unscented.

**Miss Behaving** Named because snowdrops are such 'naughty' breeders, this has curious slender flowers, hanging almost like spiders from the stalk. Although related to the autumn-flowering snowdrop, *G. reginae-olgae*, she flowers in spring.

**'Lodestar'** Named for the nearby village of Lode, this has a bold, large flower with the giant habit of its parent, *G. elwesii*.

### Hyacinths at Anglesey

The yew-enclosed formal Hyacinth Garden was laid out in the 1930s and given over to a spring and summer bedding show. The hyacinths were used for spring colour right from the first year with a blue and white theme. The modern cultivars are 'Carnegie' (white) and 'Blue Star', chosen for their late flowering to tie in with public opening at the end of March.

● As the beds are manured before dahlia planting in the early summer, the hyacinths receive no additional organic matter or fertiliser.

● A flat surface, free of weeds and stones is essential for a first rate formal display. Before planting, the Anglesey beds are

Take care when staking hyacinth blooms never to pierce the bulb.

carefully forked over, levelled and raked to remove all stones.

● Hyacinths may be planted later than you think. Richard plants in December at a depth of 8-10cm (3½-4in) and spaces his bulbs about 17.5-20cm (7-8in) apart.

● The light use of a springbok rake in late January, when the tips of the bulbs are 1-2.5cm (½-1in) below soil level effectively kills any weed seedlings and removes stones which have risen to the surface.

● Hyacinth flowers may require individual stakes to achieve their stupendous military potential. Richard suspects that excessive manuring of the soil aggravates the tendency to flop, which varies from cultivar to cultivar.

● Richard uses small green split canes for staking, threading and weaving them behind the florets before pushing the end into the soil – the flowers entirely disguise the canes as they rest lightly against them. Avoid pushing the cane into the bulb or stem as this will weaken the bulb.

● Ideally, after the display has finished you should draw your hand up the flowering stem of each hyacinth and remove the spent flowers, leaving the green stem. This nourishes the bulb and helps promote the next season's flowers.

● Leave the bulbs to dry naturally in the soil until the end of May or early June. Then dig them up, dry and store them in wire racks or net bags in a cool, dark, airy place. Good air circulation is essential to prevent fungal infection.

## Tips

● Plant cyclamen, like snowdrops, when in full growth, which is when they establish best. This also ensures you avoid purchasing illegal, wild-collected plants. Wild populations of cyclamen and snowdrops have been decimated over the years and buying them encourages the trade.

● If you plant snowdrops on the slopes of a bank, rather than on the flat, you have the benefit of looking up at the flowers, and savouring their light scent. 'Planting snowdrops along the monastic fishponds was my one stroke of genius! It's dry in summer, but the ditches catch moisture in the winter.'

● Snowdrops and winter aconites (*Eranthis hyemalis*) grow in partnership under trees at Anglesey since both like the same conditions. Richard encourages them to self-sow by passing a strimmer lightly over their heads without touching when the seed pods on both plants are just beginning to burst; the wind it creates helps disperse the seeds.

# Nymans

WEST SUSSEX

Area: 12 ha (30 acres)
Soil: Sandy loam/acid
Altitude: 152 m (500 ft)
Average rainfall: 762 mm (30 in)
Average climate: Cold winters;
    hot, dry summers

The garden at Nymans, home to the Messel family since 1890, spreads north to south along the crest of a gentle slope of the Sussex Weald. Follow a woodland path in the shade of venerable rhododendrons or take the formal way through the centre of the Wall Garden and you will experience some of the excitement which Ludwig and Leonard Messel, father and son, must have felt as they added each new treasure from Asia and the Americas.

Magnolias are a speciality here and some of the finest garden forms and hybrids were first propagated at Nymans. The tradition of adding and propagating continues, particularly in the wake of the devastating storm of October 1987. But today's visitor will not see the gaps left by those hurricane winds as a negative influence. Instead, for Nymans in the long term, it became a real opportunity to diversify and enrich the garden. Little moss-filled polythene bags which hang from the branches of mature rhododendrons are a clue for the keen propagator – 'air-layering' in progress! The garden at Nymans still moves dynamically forward as it has done since the days of Ludwig Messel.

DAVID MASTERS is only the third Head Gardener to have cared for Nymans since its birth. In charge of a staff of five at Nymans since 1980, David's earlier career with the Trust included three and a half years at Sheffield Park in East Sussex and a period as Head Gardener at Beningbrough Hall, North Yorkshire. 'I have loved the range of horticulture at Nymans from my first day, but I think you need to be in a garden at least five years before you get the feel of it. I know that the way I garden here now is more appropriate than it was in my first year. I've got a super team of well-educated gardeners and we are always re-assessing things. We never assume that because something has been done in a certain way for the last hundred years, that makes it right. On the other hand, I'll never throw out an idea, just because it's an old one!'

## Bulbs at Nymans

The Messels were collectors by nature and they gardened in this same spirit. A huge variety of bulbs is cultivated at Nymans, but they are generally used as harmonious background tones for shrubs, herbaceous perennials or occasional highlights to formal bedding schemes, rather than as 'collectables' in their own right. David feels it is crucial that he perpetuate the Messels' style. He is also well aware of the time-consuming practicalities involved in growing bulbs. Consequently he is careful to extend bulb plantings in grass only where existing colonies are established, to avoid complicating his mowing regime. The Wall Garden is carpeted with a tapestry of grasses and spring-flowering bulbs and here he feels free to embroider and experiment.

## A calendar of meadow planting

The season of the Wall Garden bulbs commences in February with the snowdrops and snowflakes (*Leucojum* spp.), running through the daffodils and *Fritillaria meleagris* of March and April to the final May fling of the dog's tooth violets (*Erythronium* spp.). The bulbs grow largely in long, orchard grass, but huge drifts of erythroniums, snowdrops and leucojums, all of which appreciate moist winter and spring conditions with a little drying in summer, have strayed into informal borders under shrubs and trees. 'Many of our oldest magnolias were planted in the first decade of the twentieth century and we regularly give them a thick mulch of mushroom compost in February or March. I think the bulbs benefit too, since the soil below must be quite tired by now.'

*Leucojum vernum* and **L. vernum var. carpathicum** (20–30cm/ 8–12in) These 'spring snowflakes' resemble their snowdrop relatives, but their white, drooping bell-shaped flowers are taller, and sometimes carried in small clusters. *L. vernum* is marked with green at the point of each segment, while *L. vernum* var. *carpathicum* has yellow markings. *L. vernum* is generally the most moisture-demanding of snowflake species, but the bulbs still flourish in the light, well-drained soil at Nymans. Cultivate in conditions suitable for snowdrops, lifting and dividing while 'in the green' (in full leaf). Dry bulbs should be planted in autumn 8–10cm (4–5in) deep.

**Daffodils** As many of the old cultivars like 'Unsurpassable', 'Cheerfulness' and 'King Alfred' were planted by the Messels in the 1920s, David devotes a little time each spring after flowering to lift and divide a few of their over-congested clumps. 'We certainly haven't noticed that their occasional 'blindness' (lack of flower) is caused by anything serious, such as narcissus fly or eelworm; I put the odd problem down to old age. However, I do feel that the last few years of increasingly hot, dry summers has affected their health. Since our soil is so very light, I use a very butch bulb planter which gets new plantings at least 15cm (6in) below the ground where hopefully they are less vulnerable to exceptionally arid conditions.'

*Fritillaria meleagris* (To 30cm/12in). With its beautifully chequered, rather mysterious drooping bells of purple and

*Leucojum vernum*

*Erythronium dens-canis*, showing the peculiar 'dog's tooth' shape of the bulb.

white, this native British lily relative is normally associated with damp, open grassland on heavy, alkaline, clay soils. At Nymans, thousands of flowering bulbs delight in the light, acid greensand, even flourishing in the shade below trees. 'Never believe in gardening folklore', advises David, 'until you have tested something for yourself!' Plant *Fritillaria meleagris* bulbs dry in early autumn at about four times the depth of the bulb or from pots in spring while in full growth.

*Erythronium* **'White Beauty'** (To 35cm/14in) A particularly fine, large-flowered form of creamy-white *E. californicum* with lightly mottled brownish-green leaves and rust-red basal markings to each petal. The strongest growing of the dog's tooth violets at Nymans, it is easily increased by lifting and dividing the young offsets from the mother bulbs after flowering. Although most gardeners would be nervous of growing such choice plants in grass, yellow-flowered *E.* 'Pagoda' and *E. tuolumnense* also enjoy the Nymans orchard grass. Erythronium bulbs grow wild in deciduous woodland or damp, mountain meadow and, like lilies, the bulbs should ideally be kept just moist, even during summer dormancy. Plant in autumn, at least 10cm (4in) deep, adding plenty of organic matter such as leafmould to border soils.

## Encouraging erythroniums and fritillaries
Both the erythroniums and fritillaries have increased considerably in recent years, largely due to David's technique:

● In June, six weeks after the daffodils have finished flowering, the erythronium and fritillary seed is collected by hand. Ripening is completed by standing the entire flower stalks in jars of water in a warm shed until the pods begin to split.

● The grass is then mown and the clippings are removed.

● The seed is scattered on the ground and the grass is then mown about once a fortnight but the clippings are allowed to drop back into and feed the turf. Similarly in autumn, leaf litter is chewed up by the mower to nourish the sward; otherwise, no fertilisers are used.

● The seed germinates the following spring. David reckons his success rate is about 10 percent, but with thousands of seeding fritillaries, this is a big annual increase.

## Sowing fritillaries in pots
● If some clumps of fritillary prove particularly good 'doers', David sows their seed in trays of a gritty, well-drained, John Innes No.1 mixture and they overwinter in open cold frames. In spring the germination rate is far higher than the open-ground seed.

● The seedlings are pricked out immediately after germination, five to a 13cm (5in) pot of the same compost. They are allowed to go dormant during the summer months as the foliage dies back and water is withheld.

● During the second season of growth they may be given a dilute liquid feed, but are not potted on.

● In their third spring when the bulbs are about the size of a pea, they are planted out into the grass while in full growth. At first the effect is a little staged, but gradually the groups mesh and begin to look less contrived.

## Bulbs and tubers for sun and shade
David particularly values *Cyclamen coum* and *Nerine bowdenii* for which he has found just the right garden situations.

Erythronium and snakeshead fritillaries are not the easiest bulbs to please, but David Masters has a carefully planned grass management tactic at Nymans which helps to ensure steady annual increase, even on this light, sandy soil.

*Cyclamen coum* **'Nymans Form'** This form of early spring flowering *C. coum* is recognised largely by the superb foliage – beetroot-red below and very silvery on the upper surface with just a little 'Christmas-tree' of green in the centre. Cyclamen readily self-sow, and David takes advantage of the seed crop to spread them through the garden. 'Although we generally avoid the use of herbicides, they can occasionally be quite useful to encourage bald patches at the base of trees where the moss then takes over. We will often plant our young cyclamen out into just that sort of position and they seem to do equally well on the sunny or shady side of any tree.'

### Growing cyclamen from seed

● Collect the seed when just ripe – the seed capsules on the coiled stems will look papery and dry.

Focusing on one colour theme, with variations, achieves the most restful effect in naturalised bulb plantings, as with these crocus cultivars growing in the Lime Walk at Nymans which include white 'Jeanne d'Arc', and purple 'Remembrance.'

- Sow thinly in seed trays of gritty, John Innes No.1 compost. David adds extra horticultural grit, until the mixture feels right. Good drainage combined with moisture is crucial.
- Cover lightly with 5–8mm grit and set in cold frames over winter. Germination rates in spring from fresh seed should be excellent.
- Prick the seedlings out into individual 9cm (3½in) pots of John Innes No.1 compost when they are large enough to be handled.
- When the leaves begin to wither naturally during the summer, allow the little plants to go dormant and stop watering. Begin to water again when the new leaves push through.
- During the second season, it is useful to apply a dilute liquid feed occasionally.
- Within two to three years the tubers are ready to plant out when in full growth – in September for *C. hederifolium* or spring for *Cyclamen coum*.

*Nerine bowdenii* (45–70cm/1½–2½ft) From South Africa, this produces umbels of spidery, narrow-petalled flowers in early autumn and revels in the dry heat of south- or west-facing borders where the bulbs receive the necessary baking during summer dormancy. The strap-like leaves appear at the same time as the flowers and last until early summer.

At Nymans, this grows in a sunny, south-facing border below *Magnolia sargentiana* var. *robusta* where it makes an excellent companion for *Agapanthus* 'Headbourne Hybrids' and the filmy grey leaf of *Artemisia* 'Powis Castle'. The nerines have increased readily by production of offsets each year and David lifts and divides the clumps when flowering begins to deteriorate markedly due to congestion. This is done in March – no earlier, since he feels that the overhanging foliage of the agapanthus offers a little protection to these slightly frost-sensitive bulbs. In very cold gardens, a thick winter mulch of bark chippings could also aid over-wintering. In the open ground, David plants dormant bulbs in summer, just under the surface of the soil, again to offer a little frost protection.

### Propagating nerines

There are many fine colour forms of *N. bowdenii* available and David particularly likes 'Mark Fenwick' (syn. 'Fenwick's Variety') a tall, vigorous plant with many large deep pink flowers. He also has a particularly fine, large-flowered form which he plans to call 'George Pinney' after the elderly gentleman who gave it to Nymans. He has found it easy to propagate from the original bulb using a similar method to

*Nerine bowdenii*

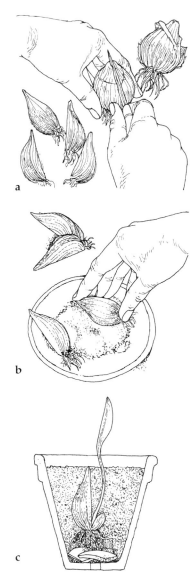

a

b

c

Propagate nerines by cutting mature bulbs into four sections. Dust each section lightly with fungicide and pot individually.

the 'twin-scaling' used for *Narcissus*. Try this with any nerine, bearing in mind that the time taken to form new bulbs will differ between cultivars.

● Take a dormant bulb in late summer, just before it comes into growth.

● Cut into four pieces with a sharp knife, ensuring that each has a portion of the basal plate attached (**a**). The basal plate will produce new roots and shoots to regenerate an entire bulb.

● Dust the base of each lightly with fungicidal powder (**b**) and pot individually into 9cm (3$^1$/$_2$in) pots of a gritty, John Innes No.1 seed compost, similar to that used for mature bulbs (**c**).

● Water immediately, but avoid waterlogging the compost – this can lead to rot. David sets pots on a greenhouse bench with gentle bottom heat to encourage roots to form rapidly.

● The bulb portions should put out new roots and foliage by Christmas and begin to form new bulbs.

● Late the following spring, when nerines naturally go into dormancy, David keeps these young plants just moist since he feels their bulbs may not have the necessary food reserves to carry them through this period of drought.

● From time to time in the second season, he applies a dilute liquid feed, but takes care not to overdo this, as he wants to encourage the root system to extend through the compost in search of nutrients.

● About one-and-a-half years after their first potting, the young bulbs should be ready to plant out in spring.

## Tips

● Try planting permanent clumps of daffodil – or any spring bulb – deeper than usual where you team them with bedding plants, so that they are less likely to be disturbed when you fork the soil to change the bedding schemes.

● Sow the seed of lilies or *Cardiocrinum giganteum* while it is very fresh in autumn. 'With its thin, papery seed-coat, it will not stand much drying and germination is very sporadic in older seeds. For lilies we use a more moisture-retentive, less gritty John Innes No.1 than used for cyclamen, and we barely cover the seed. The young bulbs are usually ready to plant out about three springs after autumn sowing. We plant them in full leaf from pots, treating them just like herbaceous plants.'

# Erddig

NORTH WALES

Area: 5·2 ha (13 acres)
Soil: Fairly light, sandy, almost
    silty loam, with some clay.
    Slightly acidic
Altitude: 61 m (200 ft)
Average rainfall: 889 mm (35 in)
Average climate: Cold, damp
    winters; warm, wet summers

Open a door through high eighteenth-century brick walls, and you enter the wonderful enclosed garden at Erddig. In early spring, its subtle framework can be appreciated: marching lines of pleached lime, orderly blocks of pyramid apple trees, and skilfully trained espaliered wall fruits.

In 1714 Erddig was bought by John Meller, a rich lawyer from London. He set about refurbishing his house and laid out the gardens in the formal Dutch style of William and Mary, which by this time was rather old fashioned. When the Yorke family inherited the estate from their uncle in 1733, they perpetuated this conservatism adding in later generations eccentricity and sheer neglect, so that the lines of the old garden were still preserved when the last Yorke, Philip III handed Erddig over to the National Trust in 1973.

The Yorkes did make some concessions to fashion in the course of two centuries. To the north and west of the house, woodland and park were laid out by William Emes in the 1770s in the style of Capability Brown. In the nineteenth and early twentieth centuries they added the formal Victorian flower garden and patterned Edwardian parterre, which sit easily with the older flavour of the formal walled garden, stretching away in lines dictated by the architecture of the house.

The only 'gardeners' bequeathed by Philip Yorke were the sheep and goats used to try to keep down the weeds around the house. So the National Trust turned to an engraving by Thomas Badeslade, made in 1739, which clearly shows the lines of the early eighteenth-century garden as their blueprint for restoration.

GLYN SMITH is the third National Trust Head Gardener to lead the massive restoration project at Erddig where he and a team of three now manage the reclaimed formal lines of the early eighteenth-century walled garden. Until his arrival here in 1985, Glyn was in charge of the smaller scale, seventeenth-century style Queen's Garden at the Royal Botanic Gardens, Kew. 'I like to think of Erddig when the first Trust Head Gardener, Mike Snowden, was rescuing it from that smother of weed and overgrown trees,' he says. 'The garden was just waiting underneath to be brought to life again. In places, while restoring the gravel paths to the exact lines of the 1739 Badeslade engraving, Mike even found the original paths intact below the turf. All that was necessary was to re-dress the surfaces. It pleases me to think that we are continually pulling it back from the decay of the twentieth century to an elegance which could have been lost for ever.'

## Bulbs at Erddig

Detailed records survive of the different kinds of fruit trees planted by John Meller in the early eighteenth century, but they reveal nothing about the bulbs. It is probable, however, that Meller and the Yorkes used the wild Welsh daffodil, the double cultivar 'Van Sion' and snowdrops for natural displays, and, given their conservatism, maintained formal lines of tulips in keeping with the Dutch style of the garden.

With the Trust's acquisition of the property, more bulbs began to arrive – almost accidentally at first. In the early days, a gift of old daffodil cultivars was made by the National Trust for Scotland from the garden at Threave in Dumfries and Galloway. And, with the demise of Rosewarne Experimental Horticulture Station in Cornwall, came further interesting old florists' cultivars, many of which pre-date the First World War and are no longer available commercially. Both collections were planted and neatly labelled, one cultivar at the base of each espaliered fruit tree, on the east- and south-facing walls. In this way the Head Gardeners have found them easiest to rationalise and maintain as named collections, and they are also undisturbed during the cultivation of adjacent herbaceous perennials.

A number of these cultivars were produced by the famous nineteenth-century daffodil breeder, William Backhouse. In their day 'Emperor' and 'Empress', now in the Erddig borders, were deemed 'two of the finest specimens known'. The result of a cross between the wild Lent lily, *Narcissus pseudonarcissus* and a naturally occurring bicoloured variety, they both flaunt splendid large trumpets, 'Emperor' entirely in yellow and 'Empress' with yellow perianth and white corona. Glyn still finds them as vigorous as ever and, with two other favourites – scented, milky-white 'Queen of the North' and the early, deep yellow trumpets of small 'Henry Irving' – has increased their number so that he can now experiment with naturalised groups in grass.

Now that the garden has moved out of the hard rescue years into an era when fine-tuning is possible, bulbs are carefully used to enhance three areas which are crucial to the bone structure of the garden. Tulips contribute sprightliness in the spring bedding schemes of the Edwardian parterre; the Old Pheasant's Eye narcissus (*N. poeticus* var. *recurvus*) and fritillaries dance in rectangles of long grass following the lines of apple trees. The wild Welsh daffodil provides a less formal flurry on the banks of the canal.

The popular Old Pheasant's Eye narcissus, *Narcissus poeticus* var. *recurvus*, is the latest of its family to flower in May and relishes the long damp grass below apple trees at Erddig.

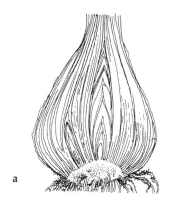

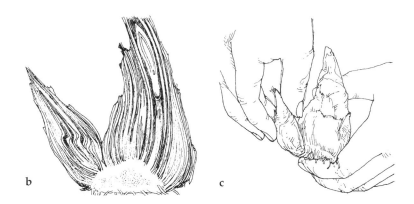

Propagating daffodils by dividing offsets. The dominant growth bud, which will produce foliage and flowers for the coming season, lies at the centre of the mother bulb (**a**). To the left is the secondary bud which will separate from the mother to form the offset (**b** & **c**).

## Daffodil cultivation at Erddig

● The daffodils are grown in three areas: in groups amongst herbaceous plantings or under trees in the Rose Garden; along the base of the old walls with the espaliered fruits; and naturalised elsewhere in grass.

● Daffodils are planted quite deeply, to the depth of one spade. Within herbaceous plantings, the gardeners plant three bulbs to a clump, with about 30cm (12in) between clumps. To guarantee a natural effect for naturalised bulbs, Glyn suggests you stand with your back to the area and lob the bulbs over your shoulder! Daffodils are always planted in early autumn, as they begin to make roots earlier than tulips or hyacinths.

● Glyn feels that the old daffodil cultivars planted along the south-facing walls, with the peaches and nectarines, are a little over-baked by the summer sun and are less vigorous as a result, even in the damp climate of North Wales. That said, he reckons it is actually quite hard to go wrong with daffodils.

● To maintain and increase their number the older, in some cases almost obsolete, cultivars are lifted and divided, on average, once every five years, depending on the vigour of the bulb.

● Before replanting, a mixture of about 50:50 leafmould and garden compost or occasionally manure and garden compost is forked into the soil. Manure would never be used on its own because Glyn feels it is too high in rapidly released plant nutrient and has noticed that bulbs grown harder – with less nutrient – are less prone to damage by narcissus fly. This pest can lay eggs in the neck of bulbs during spring and summer – the resulting grubs may tunnel into and destroy bulbs.

● Otherwise, bulbs planted in informal groups, whether in grass or borders, are rarely lifted and divided. The practice is, Glyn thinks, definitely not essential for their health. If they show signs of poor flowering they can be encouraged with a little high potash fertiliser in spring. Check for signs of narcissus fly if poor flowering continues.

Grub of the large narcissus fly feeding in a daffodil bulb.

● In the mixed borders of the Rose Garden, Glyn has used the small, sweetly scented *N. tazetta* 'Geranium', to underplant later flowering hardy perennials such as *Geranium* × *magnificum* and *G. endressii*. It is true that the daffodil struggles slightly to compete with the geranium, but he feels the effect is good enough to repeat. In addition, since the Tazettas (which include popular florists' varieties like 'Soleil d'Or' see p.37) come from the Mediterranean and prefer summer warmth and drought, it may well be that 'Geranium' benefits from this competition during the summer.

## Daffodils and narcissus for naturalising

'I would never naturalise a mixed bag of bulbs together in any one area,' Glyn says. 'Instead I would choose a variety which I think might work well on its own – and it would usually be a *Narcissus* species or one of the smaller, more gracefully flowered older daffodil cultivars, rather than a large trumpet such as 'King Alfred'. These look best to me as wild plantings.'

If you have the space, try extending the season with your choice of daffodils and narcissus. Start perhaps, as they do at Erddig, with the Welsh daffodil in March. In between, varying slightly in timing, come the main bulk of daffodil cultivars. Almost the last to flower, in May, are the *Narcissus poeticus* forms – early 'Actaea' and the later Pheasant's Eye, *N. poeticus* var. *recurvus*. As these differ little in appearance, but slightly in flowering time, a mixture of the two in the same drift will extend its flowering by two weeks. Last to flower in May are the Jonquils.

Although daffodils compete well in long swards composed of standard fine lawn grasses, Glyn believes they are less successful when surrounded by tougher field grasses such as rye. The Welsh daffodils on the banks of the canal at Erddig are aided in such a situation by the encouragement and self-sowing of wildflowers like red clover, spignel (*Meum athamanticum*) and bird's foot trefoil (*Lotus corniculatus*) which help them to compete with and weaken the tough grasses. With the addition of wildflowers, however, the first cut of the season must be pushed back. So much so that the arrival of the common spotted orchid (*Dactylorhiza fuchsii*) on the banks is now beginning to push the first cut back into July.

*Narcissus pseudonarcissus* Lent lily (10-70cm/4-28in). A British native and adopted as the Welsh national flower, this is a very tough daffodil, but still one of the most graceful for naturalising, with small, drooping, yellow-trumpeted flowers encircled by narrow, twisted, creamy perianth segments. With a wide distribution over Europe, it varies enormously from region to region. Another form, called the Tenby daffodil

LEFT: The Lent lily,
*N. pseudonarcissus*, is usually
cream and yellow with a
slightly drooping trumpet.
CENTRE: The Tenby daffodil
is an all-yellow form of
*N. pseudonarcissus*.
RIGHT: 'Incomparabilis' daffodils
have large cups, rather than
trumpets.

(*N. pseudonarcissus* subsp. *obvallaris*), is found growing wild in Wales. It is uniformly yellow, with a less drooping trumpet.

*Narcissus pseudonarcissus* 'Princeps' (45-60cm/18-24in). Another variant of the Lent lily. Glyn likes this old, robust form with yellow trumpet and white perianth. 'Makes a change from yellow and yellow!'

'Incomparabilis' daffodils (To 45cm/18in). Hybrids of the Lent lily and *N. poeticus*, occuring naturally in the south of France. Varied in form, they are usually large-cupped and bi-coloured with a sweet scent. Glyn appreciates their curiously distinctive greenish or creamy-yellow perianth, contrasting with bright orange or yellow corona. 'Inglescombe' is a much-loved double 'Incomparabilis' form.

*Narcissus poeticus* (25-45cm/10-18in).The Poet's narcissus is typified at Erddig by the late-flowering variety *recurvus* – the Old Pheasant's Eye – with its fragrant, pure white flowers and tiny, greenish-yellow corona, rimmed brightly in red. In the wild, it inhabits moist alpine meadows. 'Actaea' is a cultivar derived from *N. poeticus*.

*N.* 'Baby Moon' (To 30cm/12in). One of the most easily natu-ralised of the Jonquils (derived from *N. jonquilla*), the small, buttercup-yellow flowers of 'Baby Moon' are held in clusters of three or four to a stem, with each tiny cup circled by a neat, rounded perianth. Coming from Spain and Portugal, the Jonquils produce very fine, grassy leaves and need a warm, sunny position like the Tazettas. 'Double Campernella' is a very old, double Jonquil.

## Old Pheasant's Eye narcissus and fritillaries in long grass

There were no apples shown as wall-trained espaliers on Thomas Badeslade's 1739 engraving  and so it was assumed when restoration began that the free-standing lines of fruit down either side of the broad, central gravel path must have been apple trees. 'When I first came here', recalls Glyn, 'you could see from the top of the garden right down to the bottom. Every blade of grass was mown. I began to leave blocks of grass under the apples unmown as very regular rectangles of long grass, not only to save on mowing, but also to enhance the formal effect and to conceal slightly the bottom of the garden.

'I am not sure if it saves us much time – when we finally do mow, there is so much grass to rake and cart away! Within the blocks, we have naturalised April-flowering *Fritillaria meleagris* and May-flowering *Narcissus poeticus* var. *recurvus*. The only real problem comes in June after these have finished flowering and before it is safe to cut the foliage back for the

Old Pheasant's Eye narcissi at Erddig are naturalised in long, very regular rectangular blocks below the nineteenth-century apple cultivars. The spring contrast between long and short mown grass forms a design feature in its own right.

health of next year's display. Then we do get complaints occasionally about the mess. But a little untidiness for a few weeks seems a small price for a very structural, easily achieved design which works from early spring until May.'

### Planting

● Both the narcissus and the fritillaries seem to flower best in damper grass, particularly where the dredgings from the pond were spread during restoration. They do manage to make a sufficiently good show on drier, lighter ground, but Glyn feels the narcissus foliage is sparse in comparison.

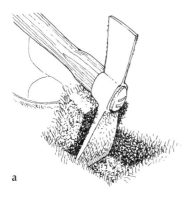

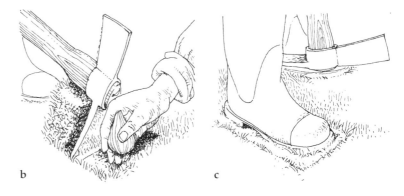

Planting narcissus bulbs with a mattock.

● The bulbs were planted in a metre radius around each apple tree, beginning about 22·5 cm (9 in) from the trunk. Weedkiller is applied when the bulbs are dormant to keep grass competition with the trees down. Glyn says, 'I did try using less competitive native meadow plants such as *Geranium pratense* at the tree bases, but unfortunately this prolonged the period during which it was impossible to mow, and we had to give up on them.'

● The narcissus were planted by gardeners working in pairs. One swung a mattock 'as deeply as he dared' (**a**), while the other inserted the bulb (**b**)! There are about 10,000 bulbs in all and the method is sometimes a little inaccurate – some bulbs are visible near the soil surface. But although they show occasional yellowing of the foliage and the odd few may rot, Glyn does not feel that flowering is affected.

● Glyn advises adding fritillaries to such a scheme a year or so after the narcissus. 'Gardeners should use *Fritillaria meleagris* more frequently – they are so cheap to buy!' Try planting the dormant bulbs in autumn, four or five to a 9 cm (3½ in) pot and overwintering in the open or a cold frame. Then plant the entire potful out in spring when both fritillary and narcissus are in growth. This way you can see exactly where to put them, and will achieve thicker, more natural clumps. Glyn has also noticed that those planted using this method are distinctly more vigorous than the dormant bulbs which he planted directly into the ground in autumn.

● If you do plant fritillary bulbs directly into open ground in autumn, plant them about 5 cm (2 in) deep. At Erddig, one gardener peels back the turf with a mattock while the other inserts the bulbs. Keeping the turf over the bulb intact (**c**) helps to prevent squirrels making a meal of new plantings.

● Thirteen years after they were planted, the narcissus have not been lifted and continue to flower well. Glyn has no plans to lift them in the near future.

### Maintenance

● The optimum time for mowing grass in which daffodils or narcissus are planted is about six weeks after flowering. But leaving the first cut until mid-July for the Old Pheasant's Eye narcissus would destroy the formality of the area, so Glyn mows in mid-June.

● The first cut leaves the grass about 10cm (4in) tall and all the cuttings are raked off and removed.

● After this, the height of the grass is gradually reduced during the weekly mowing regime to an ideal 2.5–3.5cm (1–1½in), depending on the nature of the area.

● Ideally, Old Pheasant's Eye narcissus would prefer slightly damper conditions during August when they begin to make roots and longer grass could help achieve this. But in this formal area, the grass is mown on a weekly basis until October.

● In other areas of the garden, where Glyn has naturalised the autumn-flowering crocus, *Crocus speciosus*, mowing ceases at the end of August to give the slender crocus flowers a little support from slightly longer grass during September.

## Tips

● Don't be afraid to break all the rules. If it doesn't work – only then do you know you've done something wrong!

● If you decide to naturalise daffodils in grass with other bulbs and wildflowers, try adding magenta-pink *Gladiolus byzantinus* and *Lilium martagon* with wild geranium species, poppies, orchids and other common wildflowers for mid-summer, and red *Crocosmia* × *crocosmiiflora* (montbretia) for July onwards. In practice, however, you have to draw a line in your diary for the first cut. There will always come a stage when you are heartily sick of all those seedheads and long grass!

● Really loving and growing daffodils and narcissus is essentially a bit of a collector's bug, but you don't have to go to the expense of buying named varieties. Buy a bag of mixed daffodils – the kind with the trumpets, large and small cups, doubles, and narcissus types all muddled together. Plant them out in the vegetable plot and then gradually rationalise them into their separate forms as they increase, by lifting and dividing them. Finally plant them out, one variety to an area, in different parts of the garden.

# Trelissick

CORNWALL

Area: 12 ha (30 acres)
Soil: Clay loam/acid
Altitude: 39 m (128 ft)
Average rainfall: 1,067 mm
  (42 in)
Average climate: Frost-free,
  mild winters; warm, wet
  summers

As you stand on a ridge to the south of Trelissick House, looking down over hazy, grey-green woodland of mixed oak and beech towards the steel-grey water of the River Fal, your eye could miss the garden itself, hidden in a fold of trees to the north. First you must walk to the top of the hanging valley over the river, and only then will you gradually descend through winding woodland paths until you reach the moist valley bottom and the microclimate of the stream-fed Dell. This allows the garden to shelter exotic tree ferns from Australasia or the massive, soft leaves of Chinese and Himalayan rhododendrons at its heart. You could scarcely be anywhere other than Cornwall.

This garden is deceptively young. The mild, almost frost-free climate ensured that camellia and rhododendron species and hybrids, with a fine assortment of maple, cherry, azara and photinia, grew rapidly when first planted in the 1940s and 1950s by Ida and Ronald Copeland. The neglected aspect of the Victorian parkland and garden they inherited from Ida's step-father in 1937, with its dense, gloomy growth of laurel, aucuba and invasive *Rhododendron ponticum*, was soon transformed into the Cornish speciality – a treasure-trove of spring-flowering trees and shrubs from all over the globe.

Fortunately time does not stand still for Trelissick in late May, as it does in so many Cornish gardens. Since it became the property of the National Trust in 1955, an exceptional collection of hydrangeas – over 250 types, mostly species and cultivars of the 'lacecap' persuasion – will please the summer and autumn visitor as much as do the daffodils, cherries and camellias of spring.

BARRY CHAMPION trained at Cannington College in Somerset before returning to his native Cornwall to work as Head Gardener at Tregothnan. Since 1979 he has headed a staff of three at Trelissick, who work unceasingly to maintain the health of the woody plants in their charge. No easy task in the face of the damaging gales which have crashed through the shelterbelt and tree canopy during the 1980s and 1990s, exposing many of the exotic and marginally tender species below to radiation frost and fierce, salt-laden winds. Barry rises to the challenge of such elemental battles however. 'One of the joys of this garden is that it was never designed to look in at itself, like so many gardens, but instead to look out at startling vistas over water and woodland. Cornish gardens have a very special atmosphere.'

Bulbs such as the old Victorian daffodil, *Narcissus pseudonarcissus* 'Princeps', are frequently naturalised on banks at Trelissick, here below Japanese cherry 'Shirotae'. Barry Champion finds that the technique makes for a more easily managed mowing regime.

*Anemone nemorosa* 'Flore Pleno'

## Bulbs at Trelissick

While there is no strong tradition of bulbs in this rich collection of trees and shrubs, Trelissick is essentially a woodland garden and so the daffodils and the little rhizomatous wood anemone, *A. nemorosa*, are perfectly at home whether grown in grass or informal woodland borders. 'Since I am a Cornishman – and proud of it – I'm also proud that we are probably the best daffodil growing area in the world. There is a strong historical connection between Trelissick and the daffodil too, as Ida Copeland's brother-in-law was a well-known daffodil breeder, William F. Copeland of Portsmouth. We have three or four of his daffodils growing in the garden – and I'm pleased to say they are still fine enough varieties to be available commercially seventy-five years after he bred them.'

With such a strong daffodil background, Barry is building on the presence of these old varieties and many other cultivars bred at Rosewarne Experimental Horticulture Station before its closure. There are now 150-200 cultivars at Trelissick and Barry concentrates increasingly on those which were specifically bred in Cornwall for the late winter and early spring cut-flower market. 'Since frosts are infrequent, we can speculate with some of the more tender varieties and are also building up a fine collection of Tazetta cultivars – the kinds grown in the Scilly Isles for the pre-Christmas trade in cut flowers.'

## Cultivating Cornish daffodils

At the end of the nineteenth century, Trelissick's orchards were so well-known that they were called the 'fruit garden of Cornwall'. With so many fine old varieties of apple and pear, treasured over the years for their ability to crop heavily in the tricky fruit-growing climate, it seemed natural that Barry should team these with Cornish daffodil cultivars. One cultivar is planted to each variety of fruit, in broad 2m (6ft) diameter circles of otherwise bare soil around each tree trunk.

Many of Barry's newest additions are planted in the old vegetable garden to build stock. They are given a base dressing of organic fertiliser at planting and Barry follows the feeding recommendations from Flower Bulb Research at Lisse in The Netherlands – a high potash feed in autumn, then two high nitrogen feeds at the beginning and end of April. 'It is just like growing onions,' Barry comments. 'The more nitrogenous feed you give them, the more foliage and the bigger the bulb you build up. And, in the case of daffodils, the bigger the flower too.' When his new cultivars have bulked up sufficiently they are lifted and spread to new areas any time from December to May. Traditionally daffodils are lifted in late summer, but Barry prefers to handle them after flowering, even though he may forego one season of flower, so that he can assess his additions in relation to existing bulbs.

## Recommended Cornish daffodils

**'Irene Copeland'** (To 40cm/16in) Double flowers with creamy-white outer petals and sulphur yellow inner. Still an extremely popular flower, widely available from good bulb retailers.

**'Mary Copeland'** (To 40cm/16in) Double with long, creamy-white outer petals and lemon-yellow and orange inner.

**'Mrs William Copeland'** (To 40cm/16in) Fully double white flowers. This was the nearest William Copeland came to his ambition to produce the perfect double white daffodil.

*Narcissus* 'Irene Copeland'

*Narcissus* 'Tête-à-Tête'

*Narcissus tazetta*

**'Tête-à-Tête'** (To 15cm/6in) Small, deep yellow, trumpeted flowers carried in pairs. A hardy cultivar developed through an initial cross between frost-sensitive Tazetta, 'Soleil d'Or', and *Narcissus cyclamineus*.

**'Saint Keverne'** (To 45cm/18in) Large-cupped, occasionally almost trumpet-sized, with cups indented at the rims and slightly flared. Deep butter-yellow.

**'Carlton'** (To 42cm/17in) Vigorous, large-cupped, yellow cultivar with a beautifully frilled cup. Excellent for naturalising.

## The 'Tazetta' daffodils

*Narcissus tazetta* (To 45cm/18in) Growing wild in warm Mediterranean regions, the species carries up to twenty tiny, small-cupped, sweetly scented flowers to a stem, often with a deep yellow cup (corona) and white outer petals (perianth). Little *N. canaliculatus* (to 15cm/6in) is thought to be a dwarf form of *N. tazetta*.

Some cultivars are quite frost-sensitive and may be intolerant of temperatures below $-5°c$ ($23°f$) but they have long been grown in the Scilly Isles, commencing with the earliest cultivars in late autumn and extending through to mid-spring. Best known is yellow 'Soleil d'Or'.

All require a warm, sunny position in sharply drained soil where they will receive a good 'baking' in summer. In cold areas, they are probably best cultivated in pots in a frost-free greenhouse.

**'Minnow'** (To 18cm/7in) Mid-spring. Clusters of 2·5cm (1in) wide flowers with cream perianth and pale yellow corona, fading to cream. May be shy to flower, but increases readily. Completely hardy.

**'Grand Soleil d'Or'** (To 45cm/18in) Early spring. Clusters of 5cm (2in) wide flowers with tangerine-orange corona and bright yellow perianth. Frost sensitive.

**'Pride of Cornwall'** (To 40cm/16in) Mid-spring. Clusters of two to three large, 6cm (2½in) wide flowers with deep orange-yellow corona, margined red, and white perianth. Frost sensitive.

## Managing naturalised bulbs

In such a steeply sloping garden, Barry has found bulbs particularly suitable for grass banks where they not only relish the sharply drained soils, but also help with the demanding maintenance regime. 'Banks are obviously hard work to mow regularly and, strangely enough, rough grass is never such an eyesore in those situations as it is on the flat.'

● The banks are mown with a brushcutter in late June, and the cuttings left *in situ* for a few days to allow them to dry and drop any bulb seed back to the soil. The following week the clippings are raked off and the area will only be cut once or twice more, as necessary, during the season. After the first cut, subsequent clippings are left where they lie.

● Weedkillers are used below trees and shrubs during summer while the bulbs are completely dormant. The timing obviously varies with the bulb grown, but a weedkiller containing glyphosate is sprayed directly on to vigorously growing weed foliage and the poison is then carried into its root system. Additionally, where weeds have previously been killed, a certain amount of hand-weeding may be needed later in the season.

● Organic mulches like spent mushroom compost, crushed bark, garden compost and well-rotted farmyard manure are always applied after weedkiller to suppress weeds further.

## Tips

● The essentials for bulb cultivation are good drainage, plenty of water in the growing season, and a dry rest period to encourage flower production. 'Lilies are the exception – they should be kept just moist during dormancy, but generally if you get these factors just right, you can ensure success.'

● No bulb will grow on a sour, waterlogged soil, so incorporate plenty of grit and organic matter before planting.

● Avoid dried and wizened bulbs. Buy the largest bulb you can: the larger the bulb, the better the quality of the flower. 'The one exception is the hyacinth – the blooms produced by large bulbs of 17–18cm (7–7.5in) diameter tend to topple over with the weight of their flowers.'

● 'With experience, I have come to the conclusion that an eight-week delay before cutting back the foliage of daffodils after flowering is more beneficial than the usual six-week recommendation. Natural die-back is, of course, the ideal.'

● Wherever possible, divide daffodil bulbs regularly – as much as every three years – to increase your stock and to improve their vigour and flowering.

# Knightshayes Court

DEVON

Area: 101 ha (250 acres)
Soil: Heavy, fertile, gravelly
  loam over clay base.
  Acid to neutral
Altitude: 122-152m (400-500ft)
Average rainfall: 914mm (36in)
Average climate: Mild, wet
  winters with little snow;
  warm, moist summers

Bulbs featured within the
formal lines of the Paved Garden
at Knightshayes Court include
tulips and the broad, strap-like
leaves of *Allium karataviense*,
planted to partner herbaceous
*Geranium sanguineum*.

It seems appropriate that this Devon estate whose name stems from a medieval word, 'Knyghteneheie' – probably meaning 'enclosure of the knights' – should have been graced with a magnificent, eccentric manor in grand Victorian gothic, designed by William Burges. It was the wealth from lace manufacture amassed by the nineteenth-century Heathcoat-Amorys which bought the land and built the mansion, but it was very much the creative minds of the second Sir John and his wife, Joyce, which gave us the exciting twentieth-century garden.

After their marriage in 1937, Sir John and Lady Heathcoat-Amory inherited a garden of yew hedges and south-facing terraces, designed for garish Victorian bedding. Gradually they reworked its mood with soft herbaceous and shrubby planting and a tranquil pool garden. Their greatest achievement, however, was undoubtedly the Garden in the Wood. Each year from 1950, they added an area of woodland roughly the size of a tennis court, patiently removing selected trees, high-pruning others and planting a veritable treasure trove of species until the five-acre Garden in the Wood was surrounded by a further twenty-five acres (10 ha) of gardened woodland treated in a variety of different styles.

With its formal terraces, parkland and bold swathes of naturalistic shrub and herbaceous planting beneath a canopy

of oak, pine, beech and birch, Knightshayes is not one garden, but many. Something waits for every visitor around each corner, whether they be a dedicated plantsman or a wanderer with a painterly eye.

---

MICHAEL HICKSON arrived to oversee the staff of five at Knightshayes for Sir John and Lady Heathcoat-Amory in 1963, after a seven year training in a variety of different horticultural fields. His passion for and commitment to the garden still run very deep, ensuring continued health and development even after the death of its creators. 'This garden is like an oil painting with the colours still running, fluid and malleable. I came first as a student to the painters and was finally allowed to paint myself. They were very good gardeners and our relationship was great fun. We have different areas of woodland named for us here and I can remember Sir John always used to remark teasingly that all the best plants were in "Michael's Wood" rather than "Sir John's Wood!"'

## Bulbs at Knightshayes

The Heathcoat-Amorys were never deliberate collectors of bulbs, but they used the small brushstrokes of individual plants to work up the broad, developing pictures of each garden area. 'We feel it is very important to excite the visitor's thoughts', says Michael, 'so that as you move from the carefully gardened areas of the Garden in the Wood with its delicate treasures nestling in the peat beds, you enter a cultivated woodland clearing with a mass of bluebells at your feet and feel – this is very different. Or perhaps you have a sheet of *Narcissus cyclamineus* flooding down an undulating slope to meet you and then, yards away along the path, your eye is caught by further threads of colour, drawing you round corners and on into yet another garden mood. We don't need signs and arrows – the plants tempt you along.'

## Creating habitats for woodland bulbs

The high canopy of Austrian and Scots pine, oak, beech and birch in the Garden in the Wood offer kind, dappled shade to the understorey plantings of shrubs and herbaceous plants. But as well as providing sun protection for woodlanders, the tree roots, running into areas thick with bulbs, are useful in themselves, absorbing excess moisture so that the bulbs or the tubers keep dry for their summer dormancy.

It is a delicate balance however, and a few trees are less suitable 'nurse' species for the ground floor plantings. 'Sweet chestnut is not welcome here, since it is hungry and seems to create very much more sterile conditions for ground cover growth than even the surface-rooting beeches,' says Michael. 'I also find that when the leaves drop in autumn, they do not break up quickly, but tend to cap the surface and prevent rain penetration. Similarly, birch has a very greedy mass of surface roots which rob the soil of too much moisture – fortunately we only have a few, so they cause no major problems.'

As narrow, winding paths open out into wide glades, fine foliage perennials including euphorbia, ferns, heuchera and alchemilla are planted in broad drifts to spill out under the shrub plantings in the cool of the nearby trees. This situation suits many bulbs including the coarse spring foliage of colchicums. Their partners, autumn-flowering Japanese anemones, are tough enough to push through the colchicums' leaf cover. 'We don't particularly want the colchicums in some of the more intensively gardened areas of the Garden in the Wood', Michael says, 'since the plants there are finer and more delicate, but here they work well.'

Each community of plants is finely tuned. In one area where *Narcissus cyclamineus* flower, chionodoxa are also well-established and self-sow. The foliage cover later in the season is quite heavy and the height of the plants can be as much as 90cm (3ft) or more as, for example, ferns or candelabra primulas rise to shade areas where the tiny bulbs sleep. After planting, cultivation in these areas will comprise only occasional weeding or mulching with leafmould and tidying the dead haulms of herbaceous plants in early winter.

'The bulbs enjoy a light protective canopy during their summer dormancy,' says Michael. 'The only catch is that they seed less well due to the foliage cover and I have to lift the narcissus after flowering and move them around in little clumps if I want to extend the group. This helps to create the appearance that the bulbs have spread naturally.'

A west-facing bank at the entrance to the Garden in the Wood enjoys rather different conditions although still shaded by trees from hot sun. Here two *Narcissus* species, *N. cyclamineus* and *N. bulbocodium* enjoy the moist winter and dry summer conditions they prefer. In the wild, they are most frequently found in the nutrient-poor mountain meadows, experiencing sharp drainage, combined with continuous moisture from underground streams while they are in growth. *Cyclamen repandum*, which accompanies them, is usually a plant of rocky, shaded woodland.

The soil at Knightshayes is a fertile Devon marle (a kind of heavy clay), overlying a gravelly base. Michael describes it as 'hungry' and says that leaf litter is usually rapidly absorbed into the ground. To please these narcissus on a heavier, less free-draining soil, you would need to improve drainage with coarse grit, while a lighter soil would benefit from the addition of moisture-retaining organic matter such as leafmould.

Michael says that this particular planting is a good lesson in suiting bulbs to the prevailing climate and soil of your own garden. The gradient and the tree roots here dry the soil around the bulbs during their summer dormancy. However, Devon has comparatively high rainfall throughout the year – in a much drier area of England, conditions of this kind might simply be too arid in summer for the bulbs to survive.

### Bulbs, rhizomes, tubers and corms for a woodland garden

Many bulbs, including muscari, cyclamen and snowdrops, self-sow prolifically in the borders of the Garden in the Wood. So much so, that although often the base of a tree may look grass-covered in spring, what you are seeing is in reality an artful combination of snowdrop, crocus and scilla foliage, through which the pink flowers and patterned leaves of *Cyclamen repandum* may also push. All are left to cover the ground, self-sow and then die down naturally, perhaps with a covering of fern or something rather special like the dissected foliage and deep pink, April flowers of tuberous-rooted *Geranium tuberosum* to follow on.

Michael is particularly fond of the following for gardening in dappled shade.

*Anemone nemorosa* **and** *A. apennina* Both to 15cm (6in), with March/April flowers in white or many varied shades of blue, including fine purple-violet. The long, rhizomatous roots of wood anemones love to run in moisture-retentive leaf litter and form large patches of spring colour. Summer dormant, but best when not allowed to dry out completely. Plant in autumn, just below the soil surface. Knightshayes is trialing a collection of 114 different forms of the British native, *Anemone nemorosa*, which show an enormous range of flowering times.

*Arum* **spp.** All related to our native, spring-flowering 'Lords and Ladies' or 'Cuckoo Pints', with sail-like 'spathes' folded round the sexual parts of the flower, which are carried on an erect, pencil-slim central column. In *A. italicum* 'Pictum', the beautiful arrow-shaped leaves are marbled creamy-white. Very valuable for winter to early summer foliage before going dormant in high summer and equally fascinating for its glowing red seed capsules during August and September. *A. dioscoridis* is another, rather more exotic, Mediterranean species to try, with plain green leaves and beautifully marked spathes, blotched dark purple on a pale green or deep purple

Many spring-flowering bulbs are naturally adapted to take advantage of the light, slightly dry shade offered by a canopy of deciduous trees and shrubs during the summer months. Here daffodils and bluebells flower with *Rhododendron* 'Katherine Fortescue.'

background. Plant tubers about 10-15cm (4-6in) deep in autumn, on moisture-retentive soils in dappled shade or part-day sun. As they form clumps, arums may be lifted and divided in autumn or spring.

*Chionodoxa forbesii* **'Rosea'** This March/April flowering relative of the scilla usually carries three starry, slightly larger flowers to a 15-20cm (6-8in) stem during early spring. Good for naturalising amongst dry roots at the foot of a hedge or tree. Plant in autumn about 5cm (2in) deep. Michael finds this pink form even more vigorous than the common lilac-blue and has it naturalised to run through herbaceous plants such as heuchera on glade fringes. It also looks lovely with *Scilla bithynica.*

***Erythronium* spp.** The European Dog's Tooth Violet (*Erythronium dens-canis)* and its Asian and American relations grow from small, almost tooth-shaped bulbs which inspired their common name. Flowering usefully in April and May after the main flush of early spring bulbs, they produce not only breathtakingly delicate, pagoda-like flowers in shades of pink, yellow and purple with elegantly reflexed petals, but also fine foliage, frequently beautifully mottled in dark green or brown. Plant dry bulbs in autumn about 8cm (3¹/₈in) deep and leave them undisturbed to establish in moist, leafy soils with a little overhead shade. Deep-pink flowered E. *revolutum* (to 30cm/12in) is one of the most vigorous and suitable for naturalising in large drifts, since it self-sows readily. Michael found a self-sown seedling which is particularly tall and strongly coloured with good leaf patterning and it is now known as 'Knightshayes Pink'.

***Narcissus* spp.** Also suitable for planting on rock gardens, in sun or part-day shade. These small species need a fairly cool, moist position, preferably on slightly acid soils. Will do well in short turf. Plant in early autumn at about one-and-a-half times the depth of the bulb. *Narcissus cyclamineus* (10-20cm/4-8in) Perianth swept back from bright yellow trumpets. *N. triandrus* (10-20cm/4-8in) Small, deep-cupped flowers, clustered one to six on each stem. *N. bulbocodium* (10-20cm/4-8in) Sometimes flowers in January. Delicate, almost thread-like petals and wide, funnel-shaped cup. *N. asturiensis* (5-10cm/2-4in) A miniature trumpet daffodil.

The graceful, easily grown cultivars of *N. cyclamineus,* preferably in pale colours, are used occasionally at Knightshayes just for fun, although Michael prefers to plant in natural drifts, rather than clumps. Strong-growing favourites which may occasionally need to be lifted and divided include 'February Silver', to 30cm (12in), lemon yellow and silver; 'Jack Snipe', to 20cm (8in), pale yellow and white; and 'Jetfire' to 20cm (8in), dark yellow, orange trumpet.

***Scilla bithynica*** (10-15cm/4-6in) The Caucasian bluebell has dainty blue, starry flowers in February and March. Michael values the early colour, but warns that it self-sows prolifically and must be regularly dug out where unwelcome. Plant bulbs in early autumn, about 8-10cm (3-4in) deep. Will also take full sun.

Propagating narcissus from seed.

## Species narcissus from seed

Since so many of the species narcissus and other species bulbs are expensive and difficult to purchase, searching out seed to raise your own bulbs makes sense. It also brings the added fun of variation in the size, shape – and even colour – of seedlings.

● Sow fresh seed in early autumn, filling seed trays with a soil-based, gritty, well-structured seed compost (**a** & **b**). Michael suggests sowing in rows to aid germination (**c**). 'These little narcissus are gregarious really, and I have a feeling that they help each other germinate by generating extra warmth.'

● Cover lightly with 5-8mm horticultural grit (**d**) and place the trays in a cold greenhouse or cold frame (**e**). The seed should germinate in the following February or March.

● Water the young seedlings carefully to prevent drying out or rotting of the bulblets as they develop below the compost, nourished by the whisper thin blades of foliage on the surface.

● Michael keeps the seedlings growing for two seasons by watering with foliar feed to prevent them going dormant. In this way the bulbs bulk up faster to flowering size.

● Plant the bulblets out from the seed trays in the second autumn after sowing. At Knightshayes, many *Narcissus cyclamineus* and *N. bulbocodium* flower within three years.

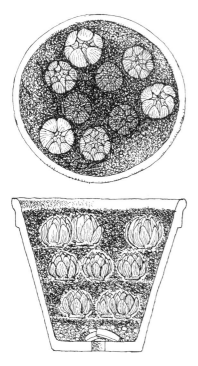

Layering lily bulbs in pots.

### Lilies in pots

For summer colour in the conservatory, Michael makes use of the exotic and highly fragrant *Lilium speciosum*, which can be plunged into the conservatory border still in its pot.

● In February, six to nine bulbs are planted in 3-litre (7–8 in) pots, using the standard, loam-based, slightly gritty, Knightshayes compost.

● The lilies go into the pots in layers, so that Michael fits more bulbs – with the pleasure of more flowers – to a pot. He puts a layer of broken crocks at the base of each pot to improve drainage and tops this with a 5 cm (2 in) layer of compost on which the first three bulbs sit. These are covered with a further 5 cm (2 in) of compost and another layer of three bulbs. There will be anything up to three layers in one pot.

● The bulbs are held in a cold frame, covered at first and then open from May onwards. In mid-summer, when the shoots are over 60 cm (24 in) tall and in bud, they are plunged to just above the rim of the pots in the conservatory borders.

● They will be watered, on average, three times a week while in growth to keep the compost moist, but not waterlogged, at all times. The bulbs receive no further feeding.

### Tips

● 'All gardeners feel at one time or another that they have done something completely wrong. Don't be put off – we lose plants as well and are always questioning ourselves as to what mistakes we may have made. We simply have to learn more about the plant and what it prefers – or detests – about our garden. Similarly, if a particular group of plants likes you, go with it. We are very lucky because the choice little narcissus and erythroniums seem to do so well for us, so I build on that.'

● Leave long grass where bulbs have seeded to dry after it has been cut, then shake it with a fork to return the seed to the soil. 'We treat the grass in which bulbs are naturalised in the parkland as hay meadow. It is then cut and spun by the local farmer in July to shake the seeds back out onto the soil.

● 'Try using the alliums or ornamental onions as much for their foliage effect as for the flowers. I have teamed the broad, strappy leaves of *Allium karataviense* with little starry leaves of *Geranium sanguineum* in a very formal area of the garden. We find, however, that we have to replace the bulbs every three or four years to maintain the foliage effect we want, since the allium leaves become progressively narrower and more wispy.'

# Killerton

## DEVON

Area: 8·5 ha (21 acres)
Soil: Very free-draining.
   Sandy loam, acidic
Altitude: 50–107 m (164–351 ft)
Average rainfall: 914 mm (36 in)
Average climate: Mild, wet
   winters with very little snow;
   warm, dry summers

*Crocus tommasinianus*, pictured here at Killerton, brings a wonderful flush of lavender-blue blooms to grass banks and wilder areas in February and self-sows in a satisfyingly prolific manner.

The big, flat-topped, pink-washed house at Killerton, Devon, nestles at the foot of the south-facing slope of Killerton Clump, a volcanic outcrop which stares out towards Dartmoor. It seems that Sir Thomas Dyke Acland, who built the house in 1778, intended it only as a temporary residence, while he laid the groundwork for a landscape in which to set a much grander mansion, worthy of a family with properties scattered throughout the West Country. But the unpretentious house remains. In the event it was to be the garden which blossomed into the real treasure of Killerton.

Six years before building his house, Sir Thomas had already employed a talented young man called John Veitch to manage and landscape all his estates. To secure his continued loyalty, he also granted Veitch permission to found a nursery at Budlake on the Killerton estate. As a result, he promoted the foundation of one of the oldest and greatest names in the English nursery trade. Over a period of 130 years, the younger Veitches would employ a succession of famous plant-hunters including William Lobb and Ernest 'Chinese' Wilson, to search out new stock for British gardens in the woodlands and mountains of North America and Asia.

Many of the first fruits of the seed they brought back from their travels were planted out at Killerton and grew at a phenomenal rate, relishing the sandy red soil and the kind, damp Devon climate of this south-sloping site. So, when the National Trust was given the property in 1944, it inherited not only a lovely, woodland garden fashioned in a meandering and informal style known as 'Gardenesque', but also an astounding assemblage of trees and shrubs, many of record-breaking size and age.

ANDREW MUDGE began his gardening career with the National Trust in 1978, working single-handed at nearby Castle Drogo. He arrived at Killerton in 1985 to manage the staff of five. 'I was born in Devon and Killerton has always been special to me. You could even say that the previous Head Gardener here, Arthur Godfrey, was my mentor when I first began gardening. It's a garden of rhododendrons and camellias – the soil and the superb microclimate, shielded from cold north winds, are perfectly suited. Although I personally have a bit of a passion for herbaceous plants, our old trees are very special friends, especially the lovely peeling, cinnamon-coloured bark of *Stewartia pseudocamellia*, the largest and oldest of its species in the country.

'A garden like this is about making the most of each view, whether it is a grand one out over the countryside towards the River Exe, or more intimate so that your management of trees and shrubs is aimed at perfectly maintaining and framing the canopy, stems and shape of each specimen like a picture.'

## Bulbs at Killerton

Planned with grass paths leading up the wooded slope, the Regency 'pleasure ground' character was enhanced by nineteenth-century drifts of crocus, snowdrops and daffodils. 'The garden is in good shape', says Andrew, 'so we can build on existing features and I am increasingly trying to improve the bulb displays which enhance aspects of the woody plant collection. We are experimenting with all sorts of new things like snakeshead fritillaries, camassia and summer snowflake (*Leucojum aestivum*), planted in natural groups throughout the woodland. But I am conscious that I mustn't overdo it. With fine views out towards Dartmoor, there are areas in the garden where the simple beauty of a vista would be destroyed by a mass of bulb colour.'

## Crocus and cyclamen naturalised in grass

The interwoven tapestry of daffodil, crocus and cyclamen on the upper slope of the Grass Path is an integral part of Killerton's spring. The crocus in particular are so happy that they have jumped the path and are running down towards the house! 'This south-facing slope brings the benefit of warm, sheltered conditions and sharp drainage which the crocus and cyclamen particularly enjoy,' Andrew says. 'If all three were to be planted on flat ground, they might be as much as three weeks to a month later in bloom.' The rather arid conditions of the warm slope helps ensure grass grows less vigorously and that bulbs are able to compete successfully.

Almost all the bulbs are planted with an old forestry tree planter – rather like a short-handled mattock with an oval base – which may be used to rip and pull back the turf with one hand, while planting the bulb with the other. The turf is then stamped back into place. With this method, bulbs are planted quite shallowly, to a depth of 5-6.25cm (2-2½in). No bonemeal is added, nor is the soil improved. 'If people saw us planting bulbs, they'd wonder if they'd ever come up! Its a fairly crude method, but it works!' Andrew laughs.

## Crocus

Premature mowing can spell trouble for colonies of natu-ralised crocus, and not only because their seeds are not ripe until June or July. Each corm lives for just one season and will

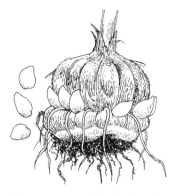

Crocus corm with a cluster of cormlets at the base.

*Crocus tommasinianus*

OVERLEAF: Cyclamen such as early spring flowering *Cyclamen coum* will often grow at the dry, hungry base of a tree where little else will flourish. Andrew Mudge at Killerton encourages their spread as a kind of ivy substitute through a judicious mowing regime.

shrivel and die during the summer – therefore it needs foliage to ensure that a new, replacement corm is produced. Many crocus will also produce a little cluster of cormlets at the base of the main replacement corm. When crocus are planted in borders, regular cultivation will accidentally break the clusters up and extend your flowering group, but in grass, thick clusters of flowers will build up around the position where the original corm was planted.

However on the Grass Walk it is the prolific self-sowing of the crocus – and the careful grass management on which this depends – that is responsible for the vast sheets of bloom, while the slope itself ensures that gravity and wind carry the dust-like seeds down the hill. Two crocus are favoured above others and planting takes place in early autumn, since these corms begin to produce roots very early.

*Crocus tommasinianus* Silvery-mauve and regularly flowering as early as January at Killerton, *C. tommasinianus* opens a delicate star-shape to late winter sun. A tendency to produce a wealth of colour variations in self-sown seedlings has resulted in the many named forms available, from the mid-purple of popular 'Whitewell Purple', to the white-tipped lavender of var. *pictus* and the dark reddish-purple of 'Ruby Giant' which will unfortunately not self-sow. Ideal for naturalising in grass, it can be a little invasive in borders, although quite valuable in that, unusually among crocus, it tolerates part-day shade. That said, sunshine is essential to bring out the best in any crocus.

*C. chrysanthus* 'E. A. Bowles' An old yellow cultivar, with delicate bronze feathering at the base. Andrew recommends the whole group of *C. chrysanthus* cultivars which are usually small-flowered, early and come in tones of yellow or cream, particularly white 'Snow Bunting' or creamy-yellow 'Cream Beauty', for their robust performance in grass.

## Cyclamen

Wild cyclamen are found in light, stony woodland, scrub or mountain pasture, often nestled in rock crevices. Few will tolerate wet summer conditions or very hot sun on their foliage and for this reason they are frequently grown under trees at Killerton, which not only provide shade, but mop up excess moisture in the soil during the winter months.

'There has been a long tradition of growing cyclamen here', says Andrew, 'as will be seen from our massive drift of *Cyclamen coum* at the base of two specimens of *Liriodendron tulipifera* – the largest tulip trees in the country. We use them as a ground cover in the barren areas below tree canopies as other

gardens might use ivy.' *Cyclamen hederifolium* and *C. coum* are the species most likely to thrive in well-managed grassland, and at Killerton Andrew actually finds little *C. coum* the stronger of the two for such situations.

Cyclamen are virtually never increased by vegetative means, so to ensure self-sowing, grass management is again crucial. Autumn flowering species such as *C. hederifolium* may take as long as ten months to ripen seed, and grass cut much before the beginning of August would limit self-sowing. As the seed ripens, it coils into itself, possibly in self-defence against passing animals and to bring it within reach of ants which disperse it, attracted by the seed's sticky covering.

Immediately after germination – usually in autumn or early winter – each seedling will produce a root and a tiny root tuber, followed later by one small, delicate leaf. It may take between two and four years for a tuber to flower – although the species grown at Killerton have all been known to flower in their second season after germination – but each will continue to increase in size and flowering capacity over many years. An elderly *Cyclamen hederifolium* tuber could grow to as much as 24cm (9½in) in diameter and produce up to fifty flowers – specimens over 130 years old have been recorded.

***Cyclamen hederifolium*** Autumn-flowering. The commonest and easiest cyclamen in cultivation. Variable in leaf and flower but most typically with pink or sometimes white, un-scented flowers, blotched purple-magenta at the mouth. Leaves are usually heart-shaped, like ivy, with patterning in grey, silver and light green, and appear with or just after flowers, sometimes remaining until the following May. Grown below trees and on the grass slopes at Killerton.

***Cyclamen coum*** Flowering December to March with scented, rather smaller and dumpier flowers than *C. hederifolium* in white, pink or magenta-purple, blotched magenta or crimson at the mouth. Less tolerant of cold wind and damp winters, but still very hardy. Rounded leaves appear with flowers, sometimes patterned in grey or silver. Will tolerate low, poor grass and is also naturalised on the slopes at Killerton.

***Cyclamen repandum*** A rarer, slightly larger, late April to May-flowering species whose large, sculptured leaves have occasionally earned it the name 'Ivy-leaved cyclamen', more commonly given to *C. hederifolium*. Scented, deep reddish-carmine flowers, typically with long, slender, twisted petals, emerging at the same time as the leaves. Completely hardy, but vulnerable to spring frosts and so Andrew grows it in areas which are very rarely frosted. Unlike the other two species, woodland shade is absolutely essential.

*Cyclamen hederifolium* showing the typical cyclamen tuber. The flowering stalks of all cyclamen are coiled in bud and again in seed.

## Managing naturalised bulbs, corms and tubers in grass

Ultimately, the rapid increase in recent years of self-sowers like crocus and cyclamen can be attributed to changes in the grass management which Andrew has made at Killerton, used for all areas of naturalised bulbs.

● The first cut will be as late as possible in July – or even into August to allow all the plants to set seed. In poor summer weather, seed-ripening is usually slow.

● The grass is left to dry, then raked away and baled for hay.

● In the autumn after leaf fall, a further cut is given and again the grass cuttings and any leaf litter are raked away.

## Planting cyclamen under trees

● In early spring while the plants are in leaf, pot-grown cyclamen may be planted out about 5cm (2in) below soil level. The covering soil should be light and friable, and a mixture of pulverised bark or leafmould could be used if necessary. The tubers are spaced about 15–20cm (6–8in) apart. Dry tubers do not establish as readily, but can be planted in July and August.

● Before planting, the soil below trees is not improved in any way, other than a light 'fluffing up' of the surface with a fork. 'The only time you might have to make changes', says Andrew, 'is when the ground below the tree is so poor that there is virtually no soil to plant into.' In these circumstances add a little leafmould and cover the tubers with a few inches of the same after planting, as cyclamen do prefer humus-rich conditions.

● Natural leaf fall helps to mimic the wild habitat of many cyclamen, but a light mulch of leafmould or bark chippings in late summer will nourish and protect the tubers as well. Although not essential for *C. coum* and *C. hederifolium*, Andrew finds that this is very beneficial for *C. repandum*.

## Tulips in the herbaceous border

Andrew finds that the many rainbow hues in which tulips are available makes them a particularly useful way of introducing an early colour scheme to herbaceous borders. Andrew's favourite lily-flowered tulip cultivars include yellow 'West Point' for the yellow and blue theme, 'Red Shine' for the central 'hot' area, and 'China Pink' and creamy-white 'White Triumphator' for the pinks and whites.

Until recently the tulips were left in the border for more than one season but Andrew found that in their second year the show was almost completely destroyed by 'tulip fire' or *Botrytis tulipae*. This fungal disease is characterised by

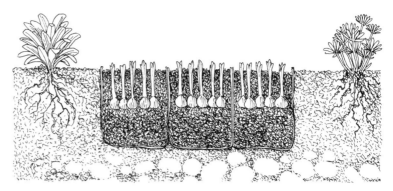

Planting tulip bulbs into containers during November to plunge into border soils in February.

spotting and distortion of the foliage at emergence and the flower buds themselves may simply wither. 'Tulip fire' may be controlled by two fungicidal sprays in late February and at the end of April, but dormant spores will remain in the soil around the bulbs. The simple remedy is to avoid growing tulips on infected soil for three years, but if – like Andrew – you are a determined tulip gardener, you may also try planting tulips in containers to plunge into the borders during early spring.

## Tips

● The method for planting bulbs is not as important as after-care. 'The soil on our slopes is pretty thin, but we never improve it and still manage to get the bulbs planted and thriving.'

● The most important ingredient is your mowing regime – don't cut too early and make sure that all the cuttings are removed to starve the grass.

● Don't ever feed grass where bulbs or wildflowers are naturalised.

● 'Adapt your planting method to the site – on our slopes a bulb planter would be useless, so we use the forestry planter and a mattock.'

● Don't worry overly about narcissus fly. 'I have seen bulbs go blind for a season, but recover full flowering health in a year or two. The damage the fly creates seems temporary. I think the affected bulbs may be encouraged to produce offsets which then come to flowering size in a few years.'

# Sissinghurst Castle

KENT

Area: 2·4 ha (6 acres)
Soil: clay/neutral
Altitude: 61 m (200 ft)
Average rainfall: 737 mm (29 in)
Average climate: Cold winters,
    often with snow; hot, dry
    summers

During the 1930s Vita Sackville-West and Harold Nicolson fell in love with Sissinghurst Castle and began the epic saga of converting the abandoned, fairy-tale tower and ramshackle farm buildings, complete with old iron bedsteads, fetid cabbage stalks and rusty sardine tins, into the beautifully wrought garden masterpiece we appreciate today. Any visitor who wanders under the cool white cloak of *Rosa mulliganii* smothering the central arches of the famous White Garden, with the ghostly shapes of verbascum, onopordum, lily and white delphinium lifting their stately heads from the surrounding borders, or is overwhelmed by the piercing perfume of Damask and Centifolia roses in the tumbling walks of the Rose Garden can testify to the superb, organised chaos of beauty which their partnership brought to the former scenes of dereliction.

Together they created what Harold liked to call Sissinghurst's 'succession of privacies'. Enclosed, geometrically shaped garden rooms are planned to open out from strong axial walks, very much as the rooms of a house open out from a corridor. Within each room – whose form was shaped by Harold's distinctively architectural eye – is a romantic profusion of planting, in the informal style which was very much Vita's hallmark. The result is a garden which was the forerunner of so much of what we now deem 'good taste' in modern gardening.

SARAH COOK trained at the Royal Botanic Gardens, Kew, and first worked at Sissinghurst under Pam Schwerdt and Sibylle Kreutzenberger, Head Gardeners to the Nicolsons from 1959. Subsequently Head Gardener at the National Trust's Upton House in Warwickshire, Sarah returned to Sissinghurst just before Sibylle and Pam were due to retire and took over their responsibilities in 1991 with the aid of Assistant Head Gardener, Alexis Datta, and a staff of six.

It is important to realise that, although the essence and spirit of the garden are retained exactly as Vita and Harold first created it, more than half of the plantings which today express Sissinghurst's mood are the result of innovations made by the gardeners themselves. Even in Vita's time, Pam and Sibylle were rarely given instruction, but simply took their cue from the existing style. As Sarah says 'Sissinghurst has always been actively gardened – rather than merely maintained – by a partnership of two minds since the Nicolsons' day. Now Alexis and I have to respond to change and be prepared to innovate in the same creative way. I can't emphasise enough that active gardening and constant evolution are what make a garden like Sissinghurst great.'

## Bulbs at Sissinghurst

The skilled use of colour which is such a feature of Sissinghurst flowed naturally from the shared vision and experience of Vita and Harold, well-documented in their letters exchanged during Harold's weekly sojourn in London. In their mind's eye were pictures of the jewel-like, clear colours of alpine meadows, or the rich poetry of deep red, purple and gold in Persian art, both of which they had enjoyed together in their travels, and they wrote frequently of translating these images to the garden's borders.

Bulbs were an important ingredient in assembling the real garden pictures on the ground. 'When you say "bulbs" at Sissinghurst', Sarah says, 'I immediately think of the Lime Walk and the Orchard'. The Orchard was where Vita played with bulbs, continually adding varieties which she had noticed in the previous season and felt inspired to grow, while the Lime Walk was Harold's special joy.

## The Lime Walk

For Harold Nicolson, politician, biographer and journalist, this was 'My Life's Work': a patchwork profusion of delectable, almost overwhelmingly glorious bulb colour, for a brief six-week period from mid- to late spring. In the same way as the diversity of colour in an alpine meadow is united by the green of the grasses, so here a myriad colours are bound together with the sharp green flowers and foliage of herbaceous *Euphorbia polychroma* 'Major', hellebore or alchemilla. Sarah feels these herbaceous plants are crucial in calming the rather busy 'bulb catalogue' effect which could easily result.

Perhaps more than any other bulb, the rich colours of tulips figure greatly in the Lime Walk's planting. But, in spite of the ideal bulb conditions of sun and warmth during spring and the drying shade of the pleached limes in summer, the annual tulip display is possible only with a heavy, yearly investment in replacement, replanting and addition. For such a thickly planted area whose residents are largely invisible below ground at the normal autumn planting time, a careful method has been devised of planting the bulbs in pots before transferring them to open ground in early spring.

## Tips for maintaining bulb displays

Sarah still uses the method devised by Pam and Sibylle , either for new groups of a particular variety or existing groups which need to be re-shaped or increased in size. Tulips are by far the most frequent bulbs to be annually 'dibbled into the border, here and there', as Sarah puts it, since they are the least persistent of all the Lime Walk bulbs. Other bulbs, such as the little *Narcissus triandrus* cultivar, 'Hawera' or the marginally tender Jonquils, may also require regular replacement, because they prove less than completely hardy in the Kent winter.

● Narcissus and most other bulbs are potted as soon as received from the bulb merchant in early autumn since they begin to make roots early. Tulips are potted in November.

● Before planting in pots, tulip bulbs are treated with a fungicide to lessen the damage by tulip fire, *Botrytis tulipae*. This also applies to occasional tulips planted directly into the open ground in other areas of the garden.

● A soil-based compost – equivalent to John Innes No. 2 – is used for potting bulbs, as Trust policy is to minimise or eradicate the use of peat-based composts.

● Bulbs are potted into pots and shallow pans of different sizes, from 9-15cm (3$^{1}/_{2}$-5in), depending on variety. Each contains a different quantity of bulbs (from one to four for larger bulbs, up to eight for smaller), so that the shape of a group in the open ground can be easily manipulated and the densities are kept uneven for greater informality.

● The pots are placed in a wooden frame and covered with 7·5cm (3in) of crushed bark over the winter.

● When leaves appear, the bulbs are removed from their pots and planted into the open ground – usually during February, provided the gardeners know that at least one week of mild weather is forecast. Occasionally the job has been left until March, but Sarah feels that the tulips have not developed so well, perhaps due to a restricted root run and lack of the moist conditions which are essential during their winter and spring season of growth.

To maintain perfection from season to season, many bulbs – especially the smallest tulip species and cultivars – are planted in containers during the autumn and transferred to the open ground in February.

OPPOSITE: This intricate tapestry of orange *Fritillaria imperialis*, muscari, snakeshead fritillary and daffodil at Sissinghurst Castle is deceptively simple. In reality the gardeners employ a time-consuming technique of planting bulbs in pots to guarantee the desired effect.

● The tulip foliage may be sprayed with a fungicide to reduce the incidence of tulip fire. Any bulb badly affected by disease or virus is removed and destroyed. For tulips, occasional slug protection with pellets is essential in wet weather.

● During flowering, there will always be spare pots to fill gaps left by unsuccessful bulbs or those which have too rapidly passed their flowering peak. A note is also made of unsatisfactory groups or desirable improvements and the necessary bulbs are ordered as soon as possible.

● The borders are deadheaded each week and the need for weeding is much reduced by the 7·5cm (3in) layer of bark mulch they receive each autumn. Sarah finds the bark mulch very useful on Sissinghurst's heavy clay soil where persistent bulbs or surface-growing types such as muscari and scilla grow, since these are easily disturbed during weeding.

● Almost every year some of the borders are stripped and replanted, and congested groups of daffodil are split in the process. Sarah estimates that each area will probably only receive this kind of careful attention once every fifteen years.

● *Fritillaria imperialis* is usually lifted and divided with the daffodils on this relatively long rotation as it is best left undisturbed while thriving. However, each season it is given a special mulch with garden compost and an extra dressing of bonemeal, because it benefits from higher nutrient levels than the vast majority of bulbs. Sarah has found also that it will not compete well with other plants and, for that reason, has died out amongst the dense ground cover plantings of the Nuttery.

## Dwarf and species tulips for the Lime Walk

These tulips are usually found wild in regions with an extremely arid, hot summer season and plenty of winter and spring rain. Gardeners who live in areas with a high summer rainfall may consequently find they are most successful when the bulbs are lifted after flowering and stored dry for the summer. Species tulips are not fussy about soil type, provided that drainage is good. On heavy soils, they may benefit from raised beds or borders into which plenty of grit has been dug at planting.

*Tulipa tarda* (8-10cm/3⅛-4in). Central Asia. Slender white flowers carried in clusters open to a striking star-shape and reveal a large, butter-yellow centre. Perhaps the easiest small species to cultivate.

*Tulipa praestans* (25-35cm/10-14in). Central Asia. Clusters of orange-red flowers. 'Fusilier' is particularly vigorous.

*Tulipa batalinii* (5-15cm/2-6in). Central Asia. Lemon-yellow

*Tulipa tarda*

*Tulipa greigii*

flowers. Hybridised with scarlet *T. linifolia* to produce fine apricot or bronze cultivars such as 'Bronze Charm' or 'Apricot Jewel'.

*Tulipa kaufmanniana* (10-20cm/4-8in). Central Asia. The Waterlily Tulip is very early, with flowers in a great colour range, although most typically creamy-yellow, stained red on the outer petals.

*Tulipa greigii* (15-25cm/6-10in). Central Asia. Prized for its broad, purple-bronze striped and flecked leaves, this has deep red, black-eyed flowers. 'Red Riding Hood' is a readily available cultivar with fine leaf markings.

*Tulipa fosteriana* (20-45cm/8-18in). Central Asia. Has large, bowl-shaped red flowers with black eye, outlined in yellow. 'Madame Lefeber' is a fine cultivar, sometimes called 'Red Emperor'.

## Tips for tulips in herbaceous and mixed borders

With the exception of snowdrops, Sarah uses the pot technique for every type of bulb or garden situation – even in the natural surroundings of the Orchard plantings into grass. 'There is always so much else to do during autumn bulb-planting time. I find I've more time to think carefully about planning border displays in January or February and then you can also actually see what is already coming up.'

● Plant groups of tulip to drift between shrubs or herbaceous perennials which are only infrequently lifted and divided, then you will rarely need to disturb them. The shrubs and perennials will function as 'nurse' plants for the bulbs, marking and safe-guarding their border positions.

● Team bulb colours with early herbaceous foliage or flowers. Sarah finds the pink or red tones of early peony shoots, lime green *Euphorbia polychroma* flowers, the reddish-pink shoots of *E. sikkimensis* and *E. griffithii* 'Fireglow', butter yellow hemerocallis foliage and soft, divided leaves of *Senecio tanguticus* particularly effective. At Sissinghurst, the purples of tulip cultivars such as 'Greuze' and 'Attila' begin the season in the Purple Border. In the Cottage Garden's hot scheme of red, yellow and orange, the two Fosteriana cultivars, 'Red Emperor' and 'Orange Emperor', with yellow, cluster-flowered 'Georgette' and deep purple 'Black Parrot' are used effectively with brilliant orange and red wallflowers amongst the sword-like leaves of iris and unfurling fern fronds.

● If planting tulips direct into open ground, plant deeply, to as much as 10-15cm (4-6in) or more, for the best chance of persistence in border soils. Tulips are particularly sensitive to soil-moisture levels during winter, and those planted too close to the surface may dry out during growth, resulting in weakened foliage, erratic flowering and greater susceptibility to disease.

## Persistent tulips for the open border

In spite of the heavy, nutrient-rich clay at Sissinghurst which tulips generally enjoy, there are only a few which Sarah knows she can count upon to persist in the borders. Although the size of flower may decrease with time, she finds these smaller flowers more graceful and in keeping with surrounding herbaceous plantings.

**Fosteriana cultivars.** 'White Emperor' (syn. 'Purissima'), 'Red Emperor' (syn. 'Madame Lefeber'), 'Orange Emperor'. All to 35cm (14in). Mid-spring. All three will settle happily, produce offsets and may require lifting and dividing as they increase.

**'China Pink'** To 50cm (20in). Late, lily-flowered, deep pink. Other fine lily-flowered cultivars include butter-yellow 'West Point' and brilliant red, yellow-margined 'Aladdin' which grows through clumps of rarely disturbed rhizomatous *Hedychium* (ginger lily) in the Cottage Garden.

**'Clara Butt'** 60cm (24in). Late, single, salmon-pink flowers. Sarah says, 'She has lived here since the Nicolsons' time and was one of Harold's favourites. To be honest, I don't know if we've just found a position which particularly suits her, or whether she would persist anywhere.'

## Alliums at Sissinghurst

The ornamental onions have proved, as Sarah puts it, 'wonderfully perennial' at Sissinghurst and are now used in far greater quantity and variety than was ever the case in Vita and Harold's day. The large, amethyst-purple globes of starry flowers produced by *Allium cristophii* (syn. *A. albopilosum*, 20-45cm/8-18in) were amongst the few which the Nicolsons did enjoy, planted to rise from the silver foliage of artemisia in the Rose Garden where they complement the mysterious dusky pinks, purples and reds of Vita's old roses. Tolerant, easily-cultivated, dramatic flowers such as these, which demand little or no 'leg-room' and happily accept a spot below drifts of herbaceous perennials are rare indeed. Autumn planting to twice the depth of the bulb in a sunny position on sharply drained soils suits them best, although they are tolerant of many soil types.

*Allium cernuum* 15-30cm (6-12in). Small, loose, nodding umbels of pink to deep purple flowers in June/July. A tremendous self-sower which accidentally placed itself amongst

*Tulipa fosteriana* cultivars are very persistent in the open ground.

*Allium cristophii*

White snakeshead fritillaries, *Fritillaria meleagris alba*, partner muscari in plantings at Sissinghurst Castle.

the young leaves of Japanese anemones in the Rose Garden. The trick was then deliberately repeated by the gardeners. An ideal partnership, since the fading foliage of the allium is disguised by the growing anemone leaves.

*Allium aflatunense* To 1m (3¹⁄₄ft). With huge, purple drumstick flowers as much as 10-12cm (4-4³⁄₄in) in diameter this is useful for May and June colour, although the tall foliage can be a nuisance after flowering. For this reason, Pam and Sibylle interplanted the bulbs through drifts of hostas in the Rose Garden. Clumps of later-flowering agapanthus would offer equally suitable allium disguise. Cultivar 'Purple Sensation' is a very similar, reliable allium which is used in the Purple Border. More reluctant to self-sow, it can be useful where the prolific habits of its relatives have proved a nuisance.

*Allium schubertii* 30-45cm (12-18in). Huge, loose umbels of pale purple flowers, as much as 45cm (18in) across in early summer. 'It jumps out to startle people from under the skirts of the old *Hoheria lyallii* against the wall in the lower courtyard below which it was planted!' laughs Sarah. Although Sarah has found the bulbs of *A. schubertii* completely hardy, sometimes a north-east wind and cruel down-draughts from the adjacent tower, or late frost in spring shrivels the foliage and flowers. She feels that it might benefit from a bracken mulch in winter.

Dusky *Fritillaria pyrenaica* thrives in a cool, moist situation at Sissinghurst Castle.

*Allium flavum* 5-20cm (2-12in) Loose umbels of pendent, bell-shaped, yellow flowers in May, turning upwards in seed. Associates with the yellows and reds of the Cottage Garden.

*Allium moly* 15-25cm (16-10in). Produces yellow, hemispherical flowerheads in May and self-sows prolifically. Suitable for wilder areas and, unusually for alliums, tolerant of part shade. Used in the Nuttery tapestry of ground cover plantings where green, white and yellow predominate.

### Hints for ornamental onions

● Sarah is tough on deadheading and weeding out unwanted seedlings – essential to curb the weedy habits of many self-sowing onions. Where left, self-sown seedlings usually take about three to five years to flower.

● Some species, such as *A. aflatunense*, will tolerate the removal of obtrusive foliage where necessary fairly soon after flowering. Although Sarah admits that this may lead to a reduction in the size of flowerheads for the large-flowered species, she feels that, as with the tulips, smaller flowers are actually more in keeping with the mood of surrounding planting.

### Tips

● Concentrate your spring bulbs in certain areas of the garden, don't just dab them about here and there. 'At Sissinghurst we have two areas – the Lime Walk and the Orchard – which are really "doing it" when we first open the garden in April, not just half-hearted little pockets dotted about. Where we use bulbs elsewhere in the garden, we always plan for them to flower with a friend to increase the colour impact. For instance, we might enhance the early pink and red of *Pulmonaria rubra*, *Lathyrus vernus* f. *roseus* and *Dicentra spectabilis* with pink tulip 'First Lady' in the Rose Garden. We concentrate on building up the colour in a specific area – further on in the same border, there may be no colour at all until later in the season.

● Plant bulbs deeper than the usual recommendation of one and a half to twice their depth. 'For most we feel no need to improve the soil. Lilies are the exception and we incorporate plenty of garden compost before planting. For South African bulbs such as nerine and *Eucomis* spp., which love plenty of warmth and sharply drained soils we add coarse grit. Feeding of bulbs is purely accidental – they benefit from doses of organic matter or fertiliser applied to surrounding plants.'

# Barrington Court

SOMERSET

Area: 4.5 ha (11 acres)
Soil: Heavy loam over clay.
  Neutral to alkaline
Altitude: 20m (65ft)
Average rainfall: 762mm (30in)
Average climate: Mild, damp
  winters with heavy frosts;
  warm, moist summers

Twenty-five miles from the coast and tucked sleepily into a fold of the Somerset countryside, lies the honey-coloured, sixteenth-century manor of Barrington Court. In 1907, when the old house and its accompanying seventeenth-century brick stable block, known as the Strode House, were donated to the National Trust, no trace of a garden remained and chickens roosted where wealthy Elizabethans had once feasted. But from 1920 until 1991 the tenancy of the Lyle family, of Tate and Lyle fame, brought many exciting changes and transformed this Ham stone treasure into a property which now also boasts one of the finest gardens to be influenced and partially designed by Gertrude Jekyll.

In any Jekyll garden one looks immediately for an architect with vision. At Barrington this vision was contributed by Colonel Arthur Lyle's architect, J. E. Forbes, who designed the vast garden walls in local stone, capped with the same fine Ham stone as the house. He also planned the exquisitely patterned brick paving in the Arts and Crafts style beloved by Jekyll. The whole mood of that style is nurtured by the Trust today in the contrast between the exact proportions and formality of a garden which speaks of wealthy owners, and the fringing, gentle simplicity of sheep-grazed Somerset cider orchards, blowing with daffodils in spring.

CHRISTINE BRAIN came to the National Trust with a gardening staff of four when the Trust took over full management of Barrington Court in 1991. She had worked for the Lyle family since 1978, after completing her training at nearby Cannington College. Christine says she can well understand the excitement that the Lyles must have felt during the partnership with Jekyll and Forbes, and the garden's first blossoming in the 1920s. 'Although this is a Gertrude Jekyll garden – we are now restoring her original planting schemes in the Lily Garden and Iris and Rose Garden in recognition of that – the Lyles' great personal pleasure in this place has contributed so much to the final results we enjoy today. I have to balance these twin influences sensibly and still keep the garden moving forward.'

## Bulbs at Barrington Court

There are great drifts of spring-flowering bulbs naturalised in the cider orchards and throughout the avenues. However, the bulbs in the three acres of what Christine calls intensive 'hands on' garden at Barrington Court are very much used as a design element to enhance herbaceous and shrub plantings, in accordance with Miss Jekyll's own principles.

It is true that in the course of planning her famous colour-graded borders, she would first look at the flower colours of favourite bulbs and harmonise these with the border theme. However, Jekyll also valued summer-flowering bulbs for the contrast which their upright form and narrow, sword-like or broad strappy foliage could make against the more billowing shapes of herbaceous perennials or Mediterranean shrubs such as sage and lavender.

Christine is keen not only to reinstate and maintain plantings in accordance with Jekyll's original plans, but also to extend new bulb plantings in the Jekyll style throughout garden areas which were not primarily designed by her. She is therefore actively adding new bulbs to more recently designed areas, such as the 1980s White Garden and the mixed borders near the pergola, known simply as The Squares.

## The Jekyll bulbs

There are several bulbs which have particularly strong Jekyllian associations. All grow in the Lily Garden where they contribute to the tapestry of colour which moves from the warmest of reds and pinks, through yellows and whites before returning to the flaming shades of summer once more.

### Lilies

Gertrude Jekyll loved to use these tall, elegant flowering spikes clad in spiralling, lance-shaped leaves, as strong vertical accents in her soft border schemes.

**Soil acidity:** Most lilies prefer acid to neutral soil, but a few are lime-tolerant, and it is these – particularly *Lilium regale*, *L. candidum*, *L. martagon* and *L. pardalinum* – that do best at Barrington.

**Sun and shade:** Most like a position in full sun, with the base in cool shade – only a very few prefer more shaded conditions. The lilies used at Barrington – with the exception of *L. martagon* which tolerates light shade – fall into the first category, making them a good choice for use among lower herbaceous plantings.

**Good drainage:** Lilies demand well-drained conditions in combination with a moisture-retentive soil. At Barrington, a high water table and heavy yellow clay subsoil only 45cm (18in) from the surface might initially seem problematic. But decades of incorporating organic matter have left a crumbly, humus-rich 38cm (15in) of topsoil and, unaccountably, says Christine, the drainage seems perfect, with the soil workable only a short period after heavy rainfall.

Stem-rooting lilies produce
roots just above each bulb,
as well as below.

*Lilium candidum*

OPPOSITE: The Tiger lily, *Lilium
lancifolium*, associates well with
the hot colour schemes in the
herbaceous borders of the Lily
Garden at Barrington Court.

**Planting depths and distances:** Some lilies produce stem-
roots on the underground portion of the stem as it emerges
from the bulb. Stem-rooters generally prefer to be planted at
three times the depth of the bulb, while non-stem-rooters are
planted slightly more shallowly, at two to three times their
bulb's depth. The species grown at Barrington are planted
roughly 20-25cm (8-10in) apart and, on particularly heavy
pockets of ground, are set on a base of sharp sand.

**Planting time:** Lilies may be planted in autumn or spring
although autumn will allow the bulbs to establish roots before
the winter. *Lilium candidum* is the exception, since it produces
leaves in the autumn and should be planted in late summer.

*Lilium candidum* Madonna lily. Flowers June/July. 1-1·8m
(2-6ft). Spikes of pure white trumpets with bright yellow
anthers. Not a stem-rooter and, unique among lilies, produces
an evergreen, over-wintering rosette of foliage. Plant almost
at the soil surface where the bulb can enjoy summer heat.
Tolerates very limy soil and much drier conditions.

Jekyll originally used this beautiful lily as an underplanting
to groups of hydrangeas which lived in the raised beds surrounding the water lily pond. 'Sixty-three bulbs in all', says
Christine; 'it must have been a lovely sight.' The hydrangeas
foundered many years ago, and when orange and yellow
azaleas replaced them, the beds were refilled with an
ericaceous soil which Madonna lilies could not enjoy. Now
the Madonna lily grows in the White Garden, with a back-
drop of *Crambe cordifolia* and in partnership with *Lysimachia
ephemerum* and white-flowered forms of *Lychnis coronaria*,
*Geum rivale* and hardy geraniums. Christine admits that it
is 'always a struggle', against the tendency to suffer from
*Botrytis elliptica* or 'Lily Disease' in the damp climate.

*L. regale* Regal lily. Flowers July. 0·6-2m (4-6ft). Spikes of
white, highly scented, golden-throated trumpets, flushed
purple at the base of the outer flower. Stem-rooting and enjoys
full sun, though not suitable for extremely limy soil. This lily
is more vigorous at Barrington than the Madonna lily, probably due to its greater tolerance of cool, moist conditions. It has
successfully replaced the Madonna lilies in the slightly acid
soil of the azalea beds – proof of its easy cultivation on a variety of soil types. Also partners the slender, orange-yellow
flowers of *Hemerocallis dumortieri* in the Lily Garden.

*L. pardalinum* Leopard lily. Flowers July, to nearly 1·8m (6ft).
Spikes of pendant, yellowish-orange 'turk's cap' flowers,
speckled and blotched in purple and shading to red at the
petal tips. Not a stem-rooter, with creeping, almost rhizome-
like bulbs which can colonise small areas in a border if suited.

These may be lifted, broken up and divided to make more in late summer or early autumn. Enjoys fairly moist conditions, but is tough enough to naturalise in a semi-wild setting. Partners orange heleniums, orange *Rudbeckia newmannii* and the yellow daisies of *Buphthalmum salicifolium* in the Lily Garden.

**L. martagon** Martagon lily. June/July. 1·5–2 m (5–6¹/₂ ft). Spikes of 'turk's cap' flowers in pink and purple, spotted in darker shades. Stem-rooting. A surprisingly tolerant species which may be naturalised. The only lily used at Barrington which normally enjoys the light, dappled shade of deciduous trees and shrubs. In the Lily Garden it grows at the feet of *Cotinus coggygria* with a fringe of bergenias.

## Crinums

The elder statesmen of the Lily Garden, the crinums in the raised beds are the only surviving bulbs from the original Jekyll plantings. They supply strongly architectural foliage at the garden's heart, as well as a dash of pink to carry her colour scheme through until autumn. 'Those old bulbs now form a massive, seething mound', Christine comments with a touch of awe. 'Like perennial Welsh onions, the same bulbs simply grow larger and produce more flowering stems each year'. Now, about seventy years after planting, they average 5–8 cm (2–3 in) in girth, running down the whole 45 cm (18 in) depth of the bed and are actually pushing the walls out! Crinums flower best if left undisturbed and when these old bulbs are lifted in the course of the garden's restoration, Christine is sure that the gardeners will be forced to dismantle the beds.

Through the crinums push – miraculously – the flowers of orange and yellow *Fritillaria imperialis* (Crown Imperials) in spring. Although not a Jekyll inspiration, this convenient association would have been to her taste, since the fritillarias give an early blast of April flower, while the foliage has entirely faded by the summer crinum 'encore'. The bulbs receive an occasional dressing of a balanced fertiliser, but are never mulched. Christine does, however, cut the crinum foliage back a little in the autumn, leaving about 15 cm (6 in) of top growth to offer the bulbs some protection over winter.

**Crinum × powellii** August/September. 60–90 cm (2–3 ft). Broad, strap-like, glossy green leaves, from which rise clusters of large, funnel-shaped, scented pink flowers on stout stems. C. × *powellii* is the hardiest of this largely tropical genus. Best in mild gardens at the foot of south or west facing walls, perhaps with a protective cover of bracken in winter. Plant in spring, approximately 30–45 cm (12–18 in) apart, with the neck of each bulb just protruding above the soil.

*Crinum × powellii*

## Companion bulbs for herbaceous and mixed borders

Elsewhere in the garden, Christine has used other bulbs which seem to team well with herbaceous plants and evoke the Jekyllian style.

*Camassia cusickii* May. 1m (3¼ft). Tall spikes of starry, pale blue flowers from a basal rosette. Best on heavy, moisture-retentive soil. Plant about 10cm (4in) deep in autumn. Christine has camassias growing vigorously in The Squares to give early colour where roses and sweet peas predominate later. *Geranium pratense* 'Mrs Kendall Clark' and *Penstemon* 'Apple Blossom' grow up in front to cover the gap left by the bulbs in the summer. Biennially flowering, dusky mauve *Delphinium requienii* and perennials such as *Lychnis coronaria*, *Dictamnus albus* and *Campanula lactiflora* – whose long stems are allowed to drop forward over the bulbs as they die back – have also made good associates.

*Galtonia candicans* Late July. To 1·5m (5ft). Long, bright green, strap-like leaves and loose spikes of drooping, milk-white flowers which make it a perfect candidate for White Garden plantings where it partners Solomon's seal (*Polygonatum* × *hybridum*) and rises through clouds of late, hazy white blossom from *Gaura lindheimeri*. It enjoys the same conditions as the lilies, with feet in moisture-retentive, rich soil and head in the sun, although it can do very well on lighter, acidic soils. In cold gardens galtonias occasionally need to be lifted and stored dry for the winter. Plant about 15cm (6in) deep in spring.

*Gladiolus* **'The Bride'** June. 45-60cm (18in-2ft). Each flower in the spike has green markings on the lower petals. Belonging to the 'Nanus' or dwarf gladioli which are possibly the most graceful and certainly the hardiest in the family. One of the best methods for establishing these bulbs of borderline hardiness is to buy them in autumn, pot up and overwinter under glass. Keep them just moist and plant out in May. Plant dry bulbs about 10cm (4in) deep. Christine finds they persist successfully in the hottest, sunniest, but still very moisture-retentive borders of the White Garden where she grows them with *Hosta sieboldiana* and *Eryngium giganteum*.

## Propagating lilies

Lily bulbs are comprised of numerous fleshy scales attached to a basal plate. The point at which the scale is attached will generate new bulblets if separated from the mother bulb, a process known as scaling. 'We do this mainly with *L. pardilinum* and *L. regale* since they do well for us, but it is worth trying to scale any lily which does well in your garden.'

Lily scaling. Lilies are very
easy to propagate by removing
individual scales from the
mother bulb. Each scale will
produce young roots and shoots,
eventually increasing in size to
form a flowering bulb.

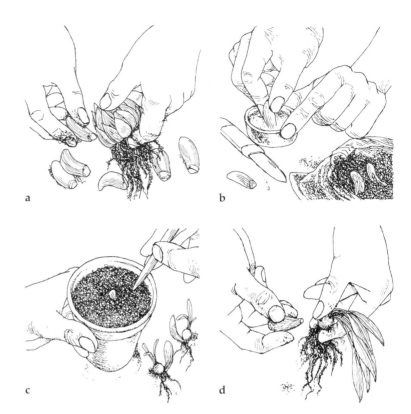

a

b

c

d

● In autumn, dig up the lily bulb and break a quantity of
scales away carefully (**a**). Christine likes to leave a basal plate
of at least 2·5cm (1in) in diameter, for the health of the mother
bulb. On average, that allows the removal of approximately
six scales. Immediately replant the mother bulb.

● Trim the scale base neatly with a sharp knife and dip in
hormone rooting powder – which also contains a fungicide –
to prevent fungal infections (**b**).

● Use a moist peat or a peat substitute and mix this with the
lily scales in a plastic bag. Hang them up in a cool, dark shed.

● Check regularly for young roots and bulblets. An autumn
propagation should give roots by January. Christine leaves the
scales until the roots are about 2·5cm (1in) long before potting.

● Pot up each scale into a 9cm (3½in) pot of good quality,
general purpose compost so that the tip is just at or slightly
below the soil surface (**c**). Christine uses the mix she has lying
around at the time – no fancy mixes for these special plants!

● As the foliage grows, so do the individual bulblets below.
When the foliage dies back later in the autumn, remove the
scales, separate the small bulblets and pot these individually
(**d**). Planting out can usually take place in the second spring
after scaling.

Crocosmia 'Lucifer' is a corm-producing perennial whose bold sheath of sword-like leaves supply a much needed contrasting shape to herbaceous borders.

## Tips

● Look for bulb companions with foliage and flowers to complement each other. 'I particularly like the effect of snowdrops flowering through the silver-marbled foliage of *Cyclamen hederifolium*. The foliage of the cyclamen lights up dark corners in winter and they both like the same conditions.'

● Look for bulbs which will flower together or slightly overlap in flowering. 'We have a large group of *Crocus tommasinianus* through which push, to follow on, the pale blue flowers of *Scilla bifolia*.'

# Mount Stewart

## CO. DOWN

Area: 32 ha (80 acres)
Soil: Medium to heavy loam,
  overlying beach deposits.
  Acid
Altitude: 0-24 m (0-80 ft)
Average rainfall: 889 mm (35 in)
Average climate: Almost
  frost-free winters; cool,
  moist summers

The garden at Mount Stewart in County Down is massive in scale. Its ponderous rose and vine clad pergola, sombre hedging, concrete menagerie of mythical beasts, and the huge, heavy Red Hand of Ulster picked out in annual bedding, leave the lasting impression of a timeless fantasy world. After absorbing the enchanted tranquillity of these formal gardens, you may wander for hours on woodland paths circling above the lake, climbing a steep hill to look down towards the glittering water through soft shrub plantings or meandering by the stream garden and through rhododendron walks.

Although the Stewarts, Marquesses of Londonderry, had owned this land since the eighteenth century, it was not until the arrival of the 7th Marquess and his wife, Edith, in 1921 that the peculiar and quirky genius of the garden was developed. Lady Londonderry soon caught gardening fever and, as formal and woodland gardens were designed and evolved, she became an avid collector of trees and shrubs, particularly those frost-sensitive genera from the southern hemisphere which benefit from the influence of the Gulf Stream and grow to magnificent stature in Ireland's soft, moist climate.

NIGEL MARSHALL and his team of five now care for the garden at Mount Stewart, bequeathed to the National Trust in 1959. Nigel arrived in 1970 from another Trust property, Trengwainton in Cornwall, after an apprenticeship at the Royal Horticultural Society's Wisley garden. Although herbaceous plants hold a special lure for him, he says he cannot afford to have favourites in a garden of this size. 'Fortunately the Londonderrys made a fine collection of plants from Australia, South and Central America and South Africa here and, although these tend to be trees and shrubs, they fascinate me completely. Maybe I'll even be lucky enough to get down to that part of the world myself some day and see the wild counterparts of our huge New Zealand cabbage palms, beschorneria, puya and agapanthus!'

### Bulbs at Mount Stewart

Snowdrops, daffodils and crocuses are planted thickly to flower on the north lawns in spring. In autumn, *Nerine bowdenii* raise starry pink funnels to the sun on the hot, narrow beds of the house terrace and *Crinum × powellii* tone with the pastel shades predominating in Mairi's Garden. Nonetheless Nigel insists that bulbs were never a key feature in the development of Mount Stewart, although the garden still bears the stamp of Lady Londonderry's decided weakness for lilies. In the Sunk Garden lily hybrids have always flaunted their showiest colours in the blue, yellow and orange theme of the central herbaceous border, while in the Lily Wood Lady Londonderry gave her passion full rein and visitors today enjoy the spectacle of twelve foot spikes of white, highly scented trumpets from the giant Himalayan lily, *Cardiocrinum giganteum* or the pink, purple, orange and white of smaller *L.* 'Shuksan', *L.* 'Maxwill', *L. martagon* and *L. regale,* rising from a cover of fern, hosta, dicentra, meconopsis, trillium and other woodlanders.

Sadly, Lady Londonderry's passion for lilies seems a perfect example of a struggle against circumstances. 'Lilies are not well suited to our climate,' says Nigel. 'The damp, still air and high rainfall during the summer – particularly in the Lily Wood – make them very prone to grey mould and mildew, so that we must enforce a regular programme of fungicidal sprays one year in three, whenever we can see that the summer threatens to be cool and moist. Above all, I feel that most lilies would prefer to see far more sunshine than is ever their good fortune in Ireland, even those which stand a little shade in the drier conditions of the south of England.'

Now Nigel concentrates on those species and hybrids which do well in Mount Stewart's soft Irish climate and, in the Lily Wood, plants largely in the more open, sunny positions where trees or large shrubs have been removed. In contrast, the long tradition of *Cardiocrinum giganteum* in the garden is easier to preserve, since these are very successful, provided they are planted on the deeper, heavier and more fertile soils which become the norm as you move foot by foot away from the thin layer of shaley sand, typical of the beach of Strangford Lough, a stone's throw away across the road.

## Lilies for a cool, moist climate on acid soils
Tolerant, easily grown lilies which enjoy acid or limy soil and do well even in a damp climate.

'Enchantment' To 1m (3¼ft). Asiatic hybrid. Has unscented, star-shaped, upward-facing, bright orange flowers, spotted in black. Stem-rooting. Lime tolerant. Flowers June/July. Produces stem bulbils. Sunk Garden.

*Lilium* 'Ariadne' 0·8-1·4m (2¾-4½ft). Unscented Asiatic hybrid with pendant, pale orange-pink, turk's cap flowers in June/July. One of a range of hybrids bred at the Scottish Horticultural Research Institute at Mylnefield for disease resistance under cool British conditions. Other fine lilies following later in the breeding programme include 'Karen North'

Shrubs, bulbs and herbaceous plants from the southern hemisphere feature heavily both in borders and in pots at Mount Stewart.

(orange-pink turk's cap), 'Peggy North' (orange turk's cap) and 'Hannah North' (pale yellow turk's cap). Produces stem bulbils. Sunk Garden.

*Lilium davidii* **var.** *willmottiae* To 2m (6ft). A favourite old lily that has been in the garden for years, with arching stems of unscented, red-orange, black-spotted, turk's cap flowers in July. *L. davidii* itself is similar but smaller in stature. Stem-rooting. Lime tolerant. No stem bulbils. Sunk Garden and Lily Wood.

*Lilium* **'Maxwill'** 1·5-2·2m (5-7ft). Asiatic hybrid. Unscented, orange-red, black-spotted, turk's cap flowers in June/July, strongly recurved at the petal tips. Stem-rooting. Lime tolerant. No stem bulbils. Lily Wood.

*Lilium* **'Shuksan'** 1·4-2m (4½-6ft). One of the American Bellingham Hybrids with slightly scented, orange-yellow, turk's cap flowers in July, spotted brown or black. Stem-rooting. Lime tolerant. No stem bulbils. Lily Wood.

*Lilium martagon* 0·9-1·5m (3-5ft). The common pinkish-purple turk's cap lily of European mountain woodland and damp meadow is probably the toughest of all lilies in Irish conditions. At Mount Stewart, it is also grown in the white form, *L. martagon* var. *album*, and a fine dark purple, *L. martagon* var. *cattaniae*. Unscented flowers in June/July. Stem-rooting. Lime tolerant. No stem bulbils. Lily Wood.

*Lilium lancifolium* **(syn.** *L. tigrinum***)** 1-1·7m (3¼-5½ft). Old-fashioned 'tiger lily' with spikes of pendant, orange, turk's cap flowers, spotted black. The larger, brilliant orange-red flowers of *L. lancifolium* var. *fortunei* are also grown, as is clear yellow, purple-spotted *L. lancifolium* var. *flaviflorum*. Unscented; flowers July–September. Stem-rooting. Lime tolerant. Produces stem bulbils. Sunk Garden.

## Propagating lilies from bulbils

Nigel regularly builds up stock of the strongest lilies by propagating from the small stem bulbils that some produce in the leaf axils of the stem. *L. tigrinum* and some of the Asiatic hybrids such as 'Ariadne' and 'Enchantment' are good candidates.

● Wait for the bulbils to ripen on the plant – usually in August. They should be producing small rootlets at the base of the bulb. Pick the bulbils off (**a**).

● Fill a large tray or wooden box (with drainage holes) using 10cm (4in) of a well-structured compost, to which you have added horticultural grit to improve drainage. The mixture used at Mount Stewart is of equal parts loam, leafmould and grit. Nigel finds that lilies prefer a compost which does not include peat.

● Plant the bulbils 1cm (½in) deep and about 2·5cm (1in) apart in rows (**b**). Set the tray in an uncovered cold frame and keep it weed-free, taking precautions against slugs and snails in spring.

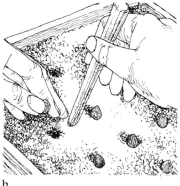

● Grow on for two years. Cover with glass and keep just moist during the wet winter months. Increase watering and give the occasional dilute liquid feed in spring and summer.

● Plant out in the third autumn or following spring when the bulbils have enlarged so that they are almost ready to produce flowering plants. Plant each bulb at about one-and-a-half to twice its own depth.

Plant lily stem bulbils to produce mature, flowering size bulbs in as little as three years.

### Cardiocrinum giganteum

The cardiocrinums are an amazing sight in full flower, with their glossy, heart-shaped leaves and 3m (12ft) spikes of drooping, scented white trumpets, streaked maroon-purple in the throat. 'We cultivate them where we can surround them with large-leaved rhododendrons or moisture-loving perennials like *Primula pulverulenta*, which enjoy the same humid conditions. Recently we have also started growing the slightly smaller variety, *C. giganteum* var. *yunnanense*, with stems and leaves flushed light purple.'

## Management of *Cardiocrinum*

The bulbs of this lily relative take some years to come to flowering size – usually when they are about 10–12.5cm (4–5in) in diameter. Then they flower once and die, so it has taken years of patient observation and skill to ensure the steady, annual succession of about twenty-four individual spikes at one time which Nigel now manages to achieve.

● Nigel usually lifts and replants a couple of dozen offsets each spring to keep the groups ticking over. Each mother bulb will produce anything from two to eight offsets.

● The ground is dug over before planting and a mixture of well-rotted manure and compost liberally incorporated, with the addition of horticultural grit on very heavy pockets of clay. *Cardiocrinum* are very demanding of soil nutrients.

● The cardiocrinums are planted differently to other lilies, with the nose of the bulb just protruding from the ground, in much the same way as a herbaceous plant.

● They are spaced about 1–1.2m (3–4ft) apart in the ground, to allow for the massive spread of their basal leaf rosettes.

● The young plants are marked with bamboo canes after planting so that they will not be trodden underfoot by gardeners working on the border, while dormant.

● After flowering the cardiocrinums are given a thick mulch of manure and well-rotted garden compost.

● In gardens colder than Mount Stewart, the young foliage in spring is liable to slight frost damage and it may be worth offering a protective covering of bracken.

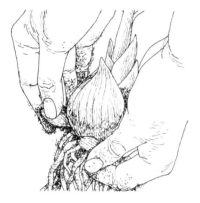

Remove offsets from a mature bulb of *Cardiocrinum giganteum* to increase your stock.

## Bulbs from the southern hemisphere

On a south-facing slope behind the lake, Nigel is able to grow plants from the southern hemisphere. Perhaps the most favoured site in this virtually frost-free garden, it offers rapid drainage combined with good winter sunlight and hot, arid conditions during summer, a perfect recipe for shrubby plants such as cistus, *Erica lusitanica*, pittosporum and leptospermum, or scented, marginally tender Himalayan rhododendrons of the Maddenii and Edgeworthii series, such as *R. lindleyi* and *R. edgeworthii.*

These are now joined by the broad, strap-like leaves and dramatic flowerheads of a varied collection of agapanthus and kniphofia forms carefully gathered by Nigel over the years. The contrast of their strong architectural form against the tiny, drought-resistant leaves and billowing shape of the shrubs ensures success on the aesthetic as well as the horticultural level. The area is relatively low in maintenance demands, receiving a simple tidy and weed in autumn and spring, coupled with a 20cm (4in) layer of weed-smothering bark chippings, on average one year in four. Gradually Nigel is adding a selection of late summer flowering plants which enjoy moisture while in growth, but produce corms or bulbs to survive periods of dry dormancy. Try these on moisture-retentive but very well-drained soils at the foot of a south or west-facing wall in mild gardens. Protection with a thick mulch of bark chippings can aid survival in areas where the plants are of borderline hardiness. In colder areas, grow them in well-ventilated, frost-free conservatories.

*Tulbaghia simmleri*

*Tulbaghia simmleri* (syn. *T. fragrans*) 45-60cm (18-24in). South Africa, sometimes surviving short periods to –10°C (14°F). Placed alternatively in the onion (Alliaceae) or lily (Liliaceae) family. Bulb-forming perennial with large, open clusters of fragrant, light to deep purple flowers and narrow, grey-green leaves smelling of onions. Nigel is fond of lilac-blue *T. violacea*, a herbaceous perennial forming almost corm-like rhizomatous roots rather than true corms, although he has lost its beautiful, rather more tender, variegated form, 'Silver Lace' and believes this is probably best cultivated under glass in most British gardens. All tulbaghias are easy to grow from seed and may be planted or divided in spring.

*Watsonia pillansii*

*Watsonia pillansii* (syn. *W. beatricis*) 50-120cm (20-48in). South Africa, usually surviving no less than 0°C (32°F). Corm-forming perennial of the iris (Iridaceae) family. Sword-shaped leaves and branching spikes of tubular, bright orange flowers rather like crocosmia in late summer to autumn. Although *W. pillansii* proves a good garden plant, Nigel has found watsonias in general quite a challenge to cultivate. The crucial point, he believes, is to assess correctly the growing pattern of each species and, from this, the optimum time for division. *W. pillansii* he now divides in late summer, since it makes new growth in autumn and winter. Divided in spring, it will simply sulk all summer. Others, like the white-flowered

OPPOSITE: The giant Himalayan lily, *Cardiocrinum giganteum*, dies after flowering. At Mount Stewart the gardeners must regularly lift and replant the small offsets produced by the mother bulbs to ensure a show of over two dozen spikes each season.

*Dierama pulcherrimum*

*W. borbonica* subsp. *ardenrei*, prefer spring division, making new growth immediately. Nigel puts this down to the quite varying rainfall patterns which different species experience in their native South Africa. 'They are definitely fussier than the kniphofias and agapanthus, preferring more moisture while in growth' says Nigel, 'although I still like to see them dry during dormancy. I have quite a few different kinds and some will refuse to flower for years until a good, hot summer – then they do the business!' Plant watsonia in spring and divide at the same time unless your plants indicate that this is not to their taste.

***Dierama pulcherrimum*** 1-1·5m (3-5ft) South Africa, surviving occasional lows of –10°C (14°F) when well-established. Corm-forming perennial of the iris (Iridaceae) family. Clumps of narrow, grass-like leaves above which rise elegant, drooping spikes of tiny, magenta-pink, bell-shaped flowers which give the common name of 'Angel's Fishing Rod'. An easily grown and delightful plant for perfectly drained, but moisture-retentive conditions. Try purple-pink *D. pendulum* and good, named cultivars such as bright pink 'Miranda', wine-purple 'Blackbird' and pale, pinkish-red 'Titania'. Plant corms 5-7cm (2-3in) deep in spring and divide at the same time.

## Tips

● A cool root-run with head in sunny, airy conditions promotes good health for lilies, just as it does for clematis. This is as true for those which produce stem roots as those which do not (see p.67). 'I find ferns make a particularly good, cool ground cover, and especially like the golden male fern, *Dryopteris affinis* subsp. *D. borreri*, with striking golden midribs in spring.'

● It is often said that the best flowering stems in cardiocrinum come from seed-raised plants, but bulbs take seven years from germination to flower. 'Try growing the plants from offsets, as we do, and you can have flowers in as little as three years.'

● Protect lilies and cardiocrinums from slugs as they emerge above ground in spring with slug pellets or a biological control. Only the initial stages of growth are crucial – once the stems are well above ground any damage is unlikely to set the bulbs back too much.

● 'We suffer little from lily virus at Mount Stewart, since I choose to grow healthy, strong-growing forms. If you do have problems, it is best to dispose of the affected bulbs immediately since the virus is transmitted to other lilies by aphids.'

# Felbrigg Hall

NORFOLK

Area: 2·6 ha (6½ acres)
Soil: Light, sandy loam.
   Neutral to slightly acid
Altitude: 61 m (200 ft)
Average rainfall: 635 mm (25 in)
Average climate: Cold, windy
   winters with little heavy
   frost; hot, dry summers

Situated close to the North Norfolk coast, Felbrigg is vulnerable to bitter North Sea winds, but the Windham family, who owned the estate from the late Middle Ages, took care to shelter the Hall and its gardens with woods of sweet chestnut, beech and sycamore.

The walls of the fine Kitchen Garden were probably built in the 1740s, the octagonal Dove-house that dominates the centre of this garden was built in the 1750s by William Windham II, but of the horticultural developments surprisingly little is known. Ironically, it is walled kitchen gardens like this that are now most fascinating to visitors. So many have had to be abandoned because of the intensive labour and expense required to maintain them. At Felbrigg the plantings have been simplified, but fruit trees are trained along the walls, flowers and shrubs brim behind box hedges, grapes hang in greenhouses, and vegetables flourish under cloches, rhubarb forcers, pea and bean tents. In the north-east sector, near the Dove-house, is one particularly eccentric partnership, as a selection of carefully tended vegetables and soft fruits flourish back to back with the National Collection of colchicum.

TED BULLOCK arrived from the commercial world of garden centre and grounds management at Syon Park in Middlesex to manage the gardens at Felbrigg Hall in 1972. He was plunged immediately into restoring the old 1 ha (2¾ acre) walled Kitchen Garden to a style which would both reflect its utilitarian past and still prove workable by the team of three gardeners which modern economic reality dictates. 'Walled gardens can be deceptive', says Ted. 'When the wind blows, the protection those walls afford is only as good as the shelterbelt which surrounds them. Ours was badly broken by the 1987 gale and I particularly dread high winds in September when our colchicum are flowering, although most years we escape the worst until the display is over.'

## Bulbs at Felbrigg Hall

The old brick walls at Felbrigg provide a perfect home for sun-loving, South African bulbs such as the scented, funnel-shaped pink flowers of *Amaryllis belladonna*, which snuggle at the foot of wall-trained apricots and peaches. Here the bulbs remain dry and warm during summer dormancy, to flower and grow in early autumn in anticipation of late season rains. The colchicum which share the garden also share the flowering season, but a mystery surrounds them since no record exists of the date of the original introduction to Felbrigg or the quantities of corms which were first planted. 'I like to think they were brought back from Italy by William Windham in the eighteenth century,' says Ted. 'It must have taken well over a hundred years for the corms to make this number of flowers.'

*C. tenorei* so visibly enjoyed the light, sandy soil at Felbrigg that it was decided to build on success. By 1984 the growing collection of eight or ten different kinds was given National Collection status, escalating to over sixty different forms by the end of the 1990s. The original *C. tenorei* remain in half-metre strips at the edge of the Double Borders, while the rest are now tended in a carefully labelled and monitored plot, with excess corms naturalised in the grass of the Orchard.

## Ideal garden conditions for colchicums

The majority of colchicum produce blooms well before their leaves during late August, September and early October. From December onwards, with the encouragement of autumn and winter rains, they begin to produce leaves which increase in size until May, when their seeds are held, ripe between the rosettes of foliage, just at ground level. Then the foliage begins to die back for a brief two months of summer dormancy, but as soon as the soil temperature drops and the rains come in late summer and early autumn, the corms become active again.

Ted says that in his experience colchicums like moisture whilst in leaf, but do not enjoy excessive heat or baking during summer dormancy – unlike *Amaryllis belladonna* or another South African bulb, *Nerine bowdenii*. 'I think that a cover of warm, dry soil – not high temperature – is the most important ingredient during dormancy. So a south- or west-facing wall will not suit them. If you add to this the fact that several kinds produce very suppressing, coarse, broad leaves in spring, you may find that they are best placed in the garden to flower at the sunniest side of large, specimen shrubs.' Those with autumn colour such as small maples, *Cotinus coggygria*, or *Rosa glauca* will be particularly effective.

'Where we have *C. tenorei* in the Double Borders, growing against smaller, sometime evergreen, shrubs, the visual effect is extremely pretty in September. However this situation is not ideal because in early summer the large leaves of the colchicum tend to press against the shrubs, excluding the light, and causing weak, elongated growth or even die-back – I then have to cut this away.'

However, Ted finds the edging of dwarf box to the border *C. tenorei* plantings is just the thing to protect the flowers during autumn winds, while those in the open National Collection plot are frequently knocked to the ground.

OPPOSITE: At Felbrigg Hall, Ted Bullock has found *Colchicum speciosum* the most robust colchicum for naturalising in grass. The flowers are well-supported by the surrounding sward even in windy conditions.

Tessellation on a colchicum flower.

Lifting and dividing colchicum corms. In the second picture, the withered remains of the old mother corm are visible between the new corm (LEFT) and offset (RIGHT).

## Tips for colchicum in borders

● Buy colchicums dry in July or early August during their brief dormancy and plant them straight away.

● In the wild, colchicum grow deeply. A mature corm of a vigorous species such as *C. speciosum* can be 10cm (4in) in length and some forms of chequered or tessellated *C. bivonae*, as much as 7·5cm (3in) in diameter. Ted plants using a trowel and since corm size can vary considerably, a safe guide when planting is to make a hole twice as deep as the corm. They can be spaced approximately 10-15cm (4-6in) apart.

● Every second year, he lifts and divides the corms in July, both to split off the young cormlets which have been produced and to check for slug damage.

● Never be tempted to remove the foliage from colchicum before it has died down naturally, as it is crucial to the growth of the corms. Therefore you obviously have to plan ahead and ensure that you plant where the large leaves of a few forms – which can grow to as much as 51cm (20in) – will not be intrusive in spring and early summer.

## Colchicum in orchard grass

Thin grassland is the natural habitat of colchicum and the heavy flowers are both supported and kept beautifully free of mud-splash in this environment – particularly valuable when growing the finest white varieties like *C. speciosum* 'Album'. However Ted finds that colchicum never increase as readily in grass as they do in borders. Additionally, with their autumn flowering and visibly coarse foliage which must remain *in situ* until June, they complicate the mowing regime to a far greater extent than spring-flowering bulbs. But the visual effect is exceptionally pretty, and Ted particularly recommends robust *C. speciosum* for the purpose. This colchicum has larger and more weather-resistant flowers than the equally common *C. autumnale*.

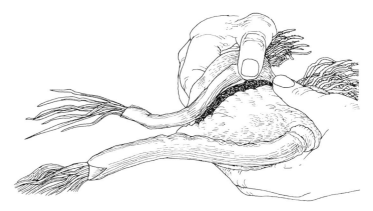

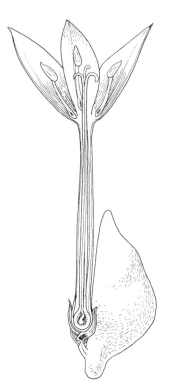

Section through a colchicum flower showing the slender tube which emerges from the small, bulging 'foot' at the base of the corm.

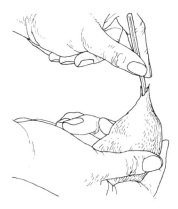

Use a small twig to dislodge slugs and eggs from the corm neck.

## Maintenance points

● Colchicum in grass at Felbrigg are planted using a spade to remove a strip of turf. The soil beneath the turf is loosened with a fork, the corm planted and the turf replaced.

● The first flowers will begin to emerge in late July and, although ideal, it is often not acceptable to stop mowing so early. Instead, the orchard grass at Felbrigg will not be cut after the middle of August and by the time the bulk of the flowers are through, the grass may be 10cm (4in) high.

● Flowering is usually over by the first week in October and the grass receives one cut on a mild day before winter sets in.

● During May, seed production occurs at the base of the leaf rosettes, only just at soil level and the leaves must be left to nourish the bulb; the first cut of the season therefore cannot take place until late June or July. Ted has noticed that colchicum take longer to die down in the orchard than in borders, perhaps due to the encouraging microclimate provided by the surrounding grass.

● During the period when the grass is left to grow long for the sake of the colchicums, Ted always ensures that a mower-wide strip is cut on a weekly basis around the entire orchard area, since this helps to maintain a tidy appearance.

● An autoscythe or a strimmer is used to cut the orchard grass in June or July and the cuttings are always raked away so that they do not rot down to nourish the coarse grasses.

## Slug attacks

Although Ted finds that colchicums are virtually trouble-free in cultivation, underground keel slugs have been declared public enemy No.1 in the Walled Garden at Felbrigg. Sparse foliage in the first year after planting may indicate slow establishment, Ted thinks. However if your plants are still patchy or unflowered in the second year, suspect slug damage. Colchicums have a foot, an elongated portion of the corm, and it is from this that the flowering tube and leaves grow. The thin, papery tunic surrounding the corm, tube and foot is the remnant of the previous year's leaf base. Slugs lay their eggs in the neck of this tunic and the growth of both flower and leaves may be destroyed if the tube is severed or the embryo leaves are nibbled by slugs. Colchicum with wide necks into which a forefinger can be inserted – for example *C. byzantinum* and some forms of *C. speciosum* – are most vulnerable.

Ted prefers not to use chemicals which might harm the thrush population. Instead he advises that corms are regularly lifted and divided every two years, not just to make more, but also to check for slugs. He uses a small blunt stick or twig carefully inserted into the neck of the corm to remove slugs and their eggs. In addition, as a precaution at planting, he may use a few granules of crushed moth ball in the base of each planting hole. Alternatively, he recommends a biological slug control.

### Recommended Colchicum varieties

Despite their common name of 'autumn crocus', colchicum are in the lily rather than the iris family to which the true crocus belongs.

*C. speciosum* **'Album'** Large, goblet-shaped white flowers, almost tulip-like. Ted describes it as the finest of white autumn flowers – worth growing for its sheer perfection of colour and shape.

*C.* **'Conquest'** Bright, lilac-rose, tessellated flowers. Tessellated colchicums are much sought after and 'Conquest' usually proves a good 'doer'.

*C.* **'Lilac Wonder'** Lilac-rose, with a long period of flower, right into October. Has very slight, variable tessellation.

*C.* **'Pink Goblet'** Finest pink, goblet-shaped flowers.

*C. autumnale* **'Nancy Lindsay'** Deep lilac stems, light mauve-violet petals.

*C.* **'Waterlily'** Large, double flowers, in amethyst-lilac. A few groups in grass can be very effective, particularly as these very heavy flowers are easily damaged in wind and rain.

*Colchicum* 'Waterlily'

### Cultivating *Amaryllis belladonna*

Growing to as much as 90cm (3ft) in full bloom and producing their strap-shaped, bright green leaves shortly after flowering, amaryllis requires heat and warmth to encourage flower bud formation for the following year and, if growing with other plants, their foliage should never overhang the bulbs and weeds must be kept religiously at bay for the same reason.

Ted only rarely lifts and divides his *Amaryllis* which flower best if left undisturbed. However when they have nosed their way up to the surface and flowering is tailing off slightly, he knows it is time to get on with the job.

● A narrow border at the base of a south- or west-facing wall is ideal for amaryllis. Divide existing bulbs in June or July when the foliage has died back.

● Excavate the soil to a depth of 46cm (18in), filling the base with brick rubble, if available, to create a limy, well-drained root run. On heavy soil, Ted thinks it useful to incorporate broken turves at the base of the planting hole as well. Mix well-rotted manure or garden compost with the topsoil.

ABOVE: The graceful, slender autumn flowers of *Colchicum* 'Rosy Dawn' at Felbrigg Hall are followed in spring by large, rather coarse leaves. Thoughtful planting is therefore essential when introducing colchicum to the garden.

ABOVE RIGHT: *Amaryllis belladonna* enjoys the base of a hot, south-facing wall at Felbrigg and prefers to remain undisturbed for a number of years. When flowering is seen to be tailing off the old clumps must be lifted and divided.

● Plant the bulbs about 30cm (12in) apart and 20cm (8in) deep. Water well after planting to encourage root formation. Ted will not replant his most elderly bulbs. 'I may be idle', he jokes, 'but I find that if I choose medium-sized bulbs rather than the largest, I will get more years of flowering from them and delay repeating this job for as long as possible!'

● The bulbs are mulched with mushroom compost to suppress weeds. 'Although I don't regularly feed my bulbs', says Ted, 'I think they would benefit from an annual top-dressing with well-rotted farmyard manure or garden compost. Alternatively, sprinkle a little Growmore around the emerging foliage in spring and fork in lightly.'

## Tips

● Sometimes dry colchicum which are already producing their flowering tubes are sold in late summer. In fact you can flower them dry on windowsills, planting them carefully afterwards. But do not buy any corms with broken tubes and, if you are planting a corm which has flowered dry or one which has already produced its tube, take care not to sever it.

● Colchicum are expensive, but most naturally increase so well that you need only buy three or five corms of a variety. Then increase your stock by lifting and dividing every two years. I expect strong growers such as 'Lilac Wonder' to double up each season. If you want to do build a good stock, however, I would advise against growing them in grass, since they will be more difficult to lift regularly.

# Plant Directory

ABBREVIATIONS
f.        forma (botanical form)
sp.       species (plural, spp.)
subsp.    sub-species
var.      varietas (botanical variety)

Heights are those of plants in full flower and are followed by time of flowering.

There are many marginally tender bulbs, such as the delicate spring-flowering colchicum or the *Calochortus* spp. from Mexico and California, which are well worth experimentation by the bulb fanatic with a glasshouse, although they have not been included in this selection.

## Late winter to early summer

Spring-flowering bulbs may begin to make roots as early as late summer and early autumn, but do not flower until spring temperatures rise. So-called 'winter flowering' bulbs (such as snowdrops) often originate in cold mountain areas and are triggered into flower by spring snow melt. In lowland gardens they flower in the relative 'warmth' of winter. The natural rhythm of these bulbs – many of which come from Europe – is most in tune with a temperate northern climate. Summer dormant. Plant dormant bulbs or corms in autumn at twice the depth of the bulb, unless otherwise stated.

*Anemone* (Ranunculaceae) Mountains and woods of Europe, south to Turkey. 10-15cm (4-6in); early to mid spring. The rhizomatous wood anemones enjoy dappled shade and cool, humus-rich soil. Plant just below the soil surface. *A. nemorosa* and *A. apennina* see page 42 (Knightshayes). *A. blanda* Produces small, knobbly tubers, rather than rhizomes. Pale blue, pink, magenta or white flowers and a good range of cultivars such as deep blue 'Atrocaerulea', pink var. *rosea* and magenta 'Radar'.

*Arum* (Araceae). See page 42 (Knightshayes).

*Brimeura amethystina* (Hyacinthaceae/Liliaceae). Pyrenees. To 20cm (8in). Late spring. Resembles a diminutive English bluebell and is worth growing in cool, dappled shade on humus-rich soil with perennials such as ferns and hostas for its very bright blue flowers.

*Brodiaea californica* (Alliaceae/Liliaceae) California. 25-45cm (10-18in); late spring. Wiry stems carry umbels of small, funnel-shaped, lavender or purple flowers, each petal marked with a darker central vein. Grow in sunny, well-drained borders.

*Bulbocodium vernum* (Colchicaceae/Liliaceae). European mountains. Flowers almost resting on soil. Mid-spring. Bright, pinkish-purple funnel-shaped flowers, like small colchicums, about 3-4cm (1¼-1½in) across. Bulb enthusiasts will want to plant it in the gritty, but moisture-retentive soil of raised beds or rock gardens with compact, non-invasive alpines.

*Camassia* (Hyacinthaceae/Liliaceae) North America. Late spring, early summer. Ideal for mixed and herbaceous borders, but will also thrive in informal shrub borders or naturalised in grass. Best on heavy, moisture-retentive soils. *C. cusickii* See page 69 (Barrington Court). *C. leichtlinii* (to 1·5m/5ft) has long racemes of starry, deep to mid violet-blue flowers, creamy-white in the form 'Alba'. *C. quamash* (20-40cm/8-16in) is a slender species, with pale to deep violet or white flowers.

*Chionodoxa* (Hyacinthaceae/Liliaceae) Glory of the Snow. Turkey. 10-20cm (4-8in). Early spring. Naturalises well around the summer-dry root systems of deciduous shrubs or can even be used to bring colour to a dry hedge base. May be planted very close together as each produces only two to three small basal leaves. *C. luciliae* (syn. *C. gigantea*) Large, starry, pale lavender-blue flowers, up to three to each stem, facing upwards. *C. sardensis* Flowers slightly smaller and deeper blue than the other two species listed. *C. forbesii* (syn. *C. siehei*, *C. luciliae* of gardens) The most frequently seen chionodoxa, it has small, purple-blue flowers with a distinct white eye, facing outwards, rather than up as in *C. luciliae*. Try also vigorous 'Pink Giant' and white 'Alba'. See page 43 (Knightshayes).

× *Chionoscilla allenii* (Hyacinthaceae/Liliaceae) Garden hybrid. To 15cm (6in). Early spring. Vigorous hybrid between *Chionodoxa* and *Scilla bifolia*. Very similar to *Scilla bifolia* and may be cultivated as for *Chionodoxa*. Deep, violet-blue flowers.

*Crocus* (Iridaceae) Mountains and meadows of Europe and Asia. 5-10cm (2-4in) Early spring. See page 48 (Killerton) for *C. tommasinianus* and *C. chrysanthus* cultivars naturalised in grass. Some of the less robust species and cultivars do best when grown on well-drained soils in sunny borders, raised beds or troughs. Also great value when plant-ed in autumn into shallow pans for an early spring pot display on the patio. *C. biflorus* subsp. *weldenii* 'Fairy' With pale, grey-lilac outer petals and white inner, this is a dainty crocus for pots or raised beds. *C. imperati* One of the earliest and most beautiful for its pale, fawn-coloured buds which open to reveal startling, bright purple interiors. Plant in pots and raised beds. *C. korolkowii* Bright yellow, shiny petals, sometimes feathered in bronze on the outer surface and opening to a flat star shape in the sun. Honey scent. Use for borders, containers and raised beds. *C. sieberi* Bright lilac flowers with a yellow throat. 'Violet Queen' is a good, deep-coloured form and 'Tricolor' is zoned in yellow, white and lilac. For borders, containers and raised beds. *C. vernus* Vigorous species from which the popular Dutch hybrids have been raised, suitable for naturalising in grass or using in spring containers. Good culti-vars include white 'Jeanne d'Arc', striped purple and white 'Pickwick', and purple 'Remembrance'.

*Cyclamen coum* and *C. repandum* (Primulaceae) See pages 52 and 23, (Killerton, Nymans)

*Erythronium* (Liliaceae) Dog's Tooth Violet. Largely European/American mountain and woodland. Late spring. See pages 44 and 21 (Knightshayes/ Nymans) The earliest to flower, carmine, rose or pinkish-purple, single-flowered European *E. dens-canis* (5-10cm/2-4in) is the most lime-tolerant species and well suited to naturalising in grass. The remaining North American species are often best on neutral to acid soil. *E. californicum* (to 30cm/12in) has creamy-white flowers and brown mottled leaves. *E. hendersonii* (to 30cm/12in) is easy to grow, but tends to remain as single plants, rather than building up into spreading clumps. Mottled leaves, lilac flowers. *E. revolutum* (20-30cm/8-12in) has very fine leaf mottling and large, deep-pink flowers. The best for naturalising in many gardens, as it self-sows vigorously and flowers reliably. *E. tuolumnense* (25-35cm/10-14in) has plain leaves and yellow flowers. Vigorous hybrids between the species are available, including yellow 'Citronella', 'Jeannine' and 'Pagoda', all of which increase readily to form good clumps.

*Fritillaria* (Liliaceae) Fascinating 'enthusiast' bulbs, curious for their sinister, drooping bells in mysteri-ous yellow, green, brown, and deep purple – and for their frequently strong, foxy scent. Many are best grown in pots in the alpine house, but the following will thrive in the open garden, on gritty, free-draining, but moisture-retentive soils, perhaps naturalised among shrubs and perennials where the soil dries slightly during summer dormancy. Add plenty of organic matter and coarse grit when planting. *F. imperialis* Crown Imperial. Turkey to Himalayas. To 1·5m (5ft). Mid-spring. Perhaps the most popular garden fritillaria, with clusters of large, brick-orange bells at the top of each leafy stem, crowned with a tuft of small, glossy, green leaves. 'Rubra' is deep red and 'Lutea' yellow-flowered. Needs plenty of sun and a warm, fairly dry position during summer dormancy. See page 58 (Sissinghurst). *F. meleagris* See page 20 (Nymans) *F. pontica* Greece/Turkey. 15-45cm (6-18in). Late spring. Grey-green leaves and green bells, flushed brown, each drooping cluster of flowers crowned with a whorl of three leaves. Easy in cool, semi-shade. *F. pyrenaica* Pyrenees. 15-30cm (6-12in). Late spring. Narrow, grey-green leaves and dark purple bells with reflexed petal tips, curled back to reveal a greenish-yellow interior. Easy in cool shade.

*Galanthus* (Amaryllidaceae) See page 16 (Anglesey Abbey)

*Hyacinthoides* (Hyacinthaceae/Liliaceae) Western Europe. 20-45cm (8-18in). Mid- to late spring. The common English bluebell, *H. non-scripta*, is well-known and perhaps not quite the garden pest that the more robust Spanish bluebell, *H. hispanica*, can become without careful thought before planting. The two differ in that *H. hispanica* is without the nodding tip to each flower spike seen in its English cousin, and has wider, bell-shaped flowers. Both will self-sow readily in moist, dappled shade and easily stray into uncolonised areas of the garden through the accidental deposit of their small bulbs on the compost heap. To prevent excessive spread where bluebells are growing vigorously it is possi-ble to remove foliage and flower spike directly after flowering without completely destroying the bulbs.

*Hyacinthus orientalis* (Hyacinthaceae/Liliaceae) Hyacinth. Turkey, Syria. To 25-30cm (10-12in). Mid-spring. Hyacinths were painstakingly cultivated and selected by Turkish enthusiasts before their introduction to Europe in the sixteenth century, when they were brought back from the court of Suleiman the Magnificent by the Habsburg Ambas-sador, de Busbecq. Like tulips, they played an important role in the foundation of the modern Dutch bulb trade. The huge range of cultivars may be used for their scented flowers in indoor bowls, outdoor containers or in bedding schemes. Left in the open ground – where they tolerate even quite dry shade – their flower spikes are never so impres-sive after the first season. Good cultivars include the rather special colourings of salmon 'Gypsy Queen', rich red 'Jan Bos' and pale yellow 'City of Haarlem'. See page 17 (Anglesey Abbey).

*Iris* (Iridaceae) The vast majority of common garden

irises, such as the popular flag irises of May and June – do not produce either true bulbs or corms, but are rhizomatous plants, very easily cultivated with the mass of summer-flowering perennials in the herbaceous borders. There are, however, two bulbous groups. Xiphium irises (40-60cm/16in-2ft) Late spring. A group of English, Dutch and Spanish hybrids best known for the contribution which the mid-blue flowers of cultivars such as 'Wedgwood' have made to the cut flower trade. Easily cultivated – and will self-sow if happy – on any average border soil in full sun where they remain slightly drier during summer. A good range of colour in yellow, blue and white makes them useful, like tulips, for colour-scheming late May/June borders.

The tiny irises of the Reticulata section (5-10cm/ 2-4in) flower as early as February and make a startlingly pretty – and often scented – show in pots, window-boxes and troughs. In the open garden they are most successful in raised beds or troughs in full sun, planted into a gritty, but moisture-retentive mixture suitable for alpines. Hot, dry, summer conditions are essential to prevent rot, but bulbs may also be lifted after flowering. Blue *I. reticulata* is perhaps the most reliable in the open garden, in a good range of cultivars including pale blue 'Cantab', reddish-purple 'J. S. Dijt' and rich blue 'Harmony'. Yellow *I. danfordiae* is the least likely to persist, with a reputation for breaking up after flowering into minute, rice-like, non-flowering bulbs. Deep planting to 10cm (4in) helps to overcome this.

*Leucojum* (Amaryllidaceae) Snowflakes. Europe, Turkey. Spring to early summer. Related to snowdrops, but with six petals of equal size rather than the three large outer and three inner of the snowdrop, snowflakes are ideal for naturalising in damp grassland or informal shrub borders. Best planted, like snowdrops, in the green. See page 20 for spring snowflakes (Nymans). *L. aestivum* summer snowflake. (30-45cm/12-18in) The tallest and latest snowflake, flowering in April and May. Petals have green tips. 'Gravetye Giant' is a vigorous form which may be 90cm (3ft) in very moist soil.

*Muscari* Grape Hyacinth (Hyacinthaceae/Liliaceae). Southern Europe, North Africa, Turkey, Iran. Mostly 15-20cm (6-8in). Mid- to late spring. Most muscari flowers are arranged in dense spikes like hyacinths, but the small, sometimes nearly spherical, flowers are constricted at the mouth. For sun or part shade on almost any soil. Common *M. neglectum*, with blue-black, white-rimmed flowers, is almost weed-like in its self-sowing habits, but is good for naturalising in large, semi-wild plantings below shrubs, as is violet-blue *M. armeniacum*, particularly in its fine, double-flowered variety, 'Blue Spike'.

Others to try include: the tufted, bright violet flowers of the 'tassel hyacinth' *M. comosum* (30-60cm/1-2ft) and *M. botryoides* – which prefers moister conditions than most – with clusters of nearly spherical, brilliant blue flowers.

*Narcissus* (Amaryllidaceae). Daffodil species are distributed throughout Europe, with the major centre in Spain, Portugal and North Africa. Often from southern mountains and meadows, the true species – with the exception of *N. pseudonarcissus* and *N. poeticus* – are generally slightly more demanding of precisely the right garden conditions than the cultivars, usually preferring very moist but sharply drained spring conditions, combined with warm, rather drier summer soils. The broad range of tall and dwarf modern cultivars are much more adaptable, but reach perfection on soils which do not dry out completely in summer. Daffodil cultivars are classified into the following groups (examples of good cultivars, in addition to those mentioned within the text, are given for each):
**Trumpet** White 'Empress of Ireland' or 'Mount Hood'; yellow 'Arctic Gold' or 'Dutch Master'; bicoloured 'Bravoure'.
**Large-cupped** With cup more than one third the length of, but not equal to, the petals: sulphur-yellow 'Carlton'; white-petalled, orange-cupped 'Professor Einstein'; white 'Ice Follies' or 'Broomhill'; bicoloured 'Daydream'.
**Small-cupped** 'Merlin' with white petals and red-rimmed, yellow cup; white 'Verona'.
**Double** Tiny yellow 'Rip van Winkle'; golden and orange 'Tahiti'; multi-headed yellow 'Cheerfulness'.
**Triandrus cultivars** Usually small, with more than one flower to a stem: lemon-yellow 'Hawera' or 'April Tears'; white 'Tresamble'.
**Cyclamineus cultivars** With the backswept petals of the species: white and pale yellow 'Dove Wings'; golden 'February Gold'; yellow 'Charity May'; white 'Jenny'.
**Jonquilla cultivars** With the fragrance and multi-headed habit of the species: yellow and orange 'Lintie'; lemon and white 'Pipit'; yellow 'Sweetness'.
**Tazetta cultivars** Yellow and orange 'Scarlet Gem'; white and yellow 'Avalanche'.
**Poeticus cultivars** 'Cantabile' with white petals and red-rimmed, green cup.
**Split corona cultivars** or so-called 'Orchid-flowered' daffodils: lemon and white 'Cassata'.
See pages 20, 29, 36 and 44 (Nymans/Erddig/ Trelissick/Knightshayes) for a further selection of species and good cultivars.

*Nectaroscordum siculum* (Alliaceae/Liliaceae) Southern France, Italy. To 1·5m (5ft). Late spring. Related to the ornamental onions and with the same strong scent, the nodding, bell-shaped flowers are white, flushed maroon and green, and held in nodding umbels of up to thirty flowers on a wiry stem. Fascinating rather than beautiful. Plant in sun or dappled shade on any soil, preferably in wilder areas, since it is a prolific self-sower.

*Ornithogalum* (Hyacinthaceae/Liliaceae) Star of Bethlehem. Mediterranean, Europe, Turkey. Mid- to late spring. Gentle spikes of silvery-white flower, marked green on the outer petals, make these restful bulbs for dappled or part-day shade, providing they receive at least some sunshine to open the flowers. Very easy to cultivate on well-drained soil. The commonest species, *O. umbellatum* (10-30cm/4-12in) naturalises well in grass. Later flowering *O. nutans* (20-60cm/8-24in) has beautifully recurved petals to each star-shaped flower and may be naturalised in grass or will thrive at the dry, partially-shaded base of a hedge.

*Puschkinia scilloides* var. *libanotica* (Hyacinthaceae/Liliaceae) Lebanon. 5-10cm (2-4in). Late spring. Similar in appearance to the scillas, carrying spikes of pale blue flowers with a darker blue stripe along the centre of each petal. For naturalising in cool, dappled shade and humus-rich soils where they do not dry out excessively during summer.

*Scilla* (Hyacinthaceae/Liliaceae) Squill. Europe, Turkey, Iran, Western Asia. 5-10cm (2-4in). Early to late spring. Dwarf bulbs – including a number of autumn-flowering species – with spikes of bell or star-shaped blue flowers. Generally unfussy about garden position, they are at their best on cool, moist soils in dappled shade amongst shrubs where they will not dry out excessively in summer. Perhaps most useful are the early, starry flowers of easy-going, deep-violet *S. bifolia* and the nodding, deep blue bells of *S. siberica* 'Spring Beauty'. Try also *S. mischtschenkoana* whose pale blue flowers, striped dark blue on the reverse, open to wide stars in the very early spring sunshine. *S. peruviana* is rather different, requiring a warm, sunny, but still moist position in summer. Produces a broad rosette of sword-shaped leaves in autumn and, in late spring, dense, conical heads of steely blue flowers to 25cm (10in). See page 44 (Knightshayes).

*Tulipa* (Liliaceae) The small, wild, species tulips come primarily from Asia Minor, with major areas of distribution in Turkey, Iran and Afghanistan. First introduced to Europe by the Habsburg Ambassador to Istanbul, de Busbecq, in the mid-sixteenth century, the rainbow colour variations, selected over centuries by the Turks, caused immediate fascination. Subsequent European developments laid the foundation for the huge modern Dutch bulb industry, which has produced an enormous range of hybrids and cultivars.

Tulips are sometimes rather transient garden bulbs, particularly since they demand a very dry summer dormancy which can be tricky to supply in the British climate. Some gardeners lift them about six weeks after flowering and dry them off for re-planting in autumn.

See page 58 (Sissinghurst) for dwarf species and cultivars. The large cultivars are usually divided into the following sections (examples of good cultivars, in addition to those mentioned within the text, are given for each).

**Single, early** Good weather resistance, to 40cm (16in) tall: apricot-pink 'Apricot Beauty'; yellow 'Bellona'; pale orange, violet-flushed 'Prinses Irene'.
**Double, early** To 30cm (12in): pink 'Peach Blossom'; coral-red 'Oranje Nassau'.
**Mid-season** To 40-50cm (16-20in): deep purple, white-edged 'African Queen'; pale and rosy-pink 'New Design'; red 'Cassini'.
**Darwin hybrids** Mid-season, 55-65cm (22-26in). Many quite persistent in gardens: scarlet 'Apeldoorn'; yellow 'Golden Apeldoorn'; yellow, orange-speckled 'Beauty of Apeldoorn'; salmon-pink, violet-flushed 'Elizabeth Arden'.
**Single, late** Tall, to 85cm (2¾ft): deep purple 'Queen of Night'; lavender mauve 'Bleu Amabile'; 'Sorbet', white with rose markings.
**Lily-flowered** Late-flowering, with elegant, long, pointed petals, 45-60cm (1½-2ft). Very popular with Trust Head Gardeners: 'White Triumphator'; reddish-purple, white-margined 'Maytime'.
**Fringed** Late-flowering, 45-60cm (1½-2ft). Fringed petals: lavender blue 'Blue Heron' with paler fringe; white 'Swan Wings'.
**Viridiflora** Late-flowering, 30-40cm (12-16in), with flowers partially green: pink and green 'Groenland'; creamy-yellow and green 'Spring Green'; salmon-pink, purple and green 'Artist'.
**Parrot** Double, late-flowering, 50-60cm (20-24in), fringed and splashed in a variety of colours: deep purple 'Black Parrot'; bright pink and green 'Fantasy'; white and deep pink 'Estella Rijnveld'; orange and green 'Orange Favourite'.
**Paeony-flowered** Late-flowering, 45-55cm (18-22in): rose and pale yellow 'Angelique'; bright red, yellow-edged 'Allegretto'; white 'Mount Tacoma'.

See also pages 61 and 53 (Sissinghurst and Killerton).

## Summer

**Summer flowering bulbs frequently come from areas such as Mexico, the eastern Cape of South Africa or the monsoon areas of East Asia where summer**

rain is plentiful, coupled with relatively cool, dry winters. Comparatively dry winter conditions are therefore usually an important factor in their successful cultivation. Plant dormant bulbs or corms as soon as received – generally in spring or early summer – at twice the depth of the bulb, unless otherwise stated.

*Allium* (Alliaceae/Liliaceae) See page 61 (Sissinghurst)

*Cardiocrinum* (Liliaceae) See page 76 (Mount Stewart)

*Crinum* (Amaryllidaceae) See page 68 (Barrington Court)

*Crocosmia* (Iridaceae). South Africa. Mid- to late summer. Since truly hot, fiery colours are always in short supply for borders, crocosmia should never be forgotten, with their added bonus of fresh, sword-like leaves to contrast with softer herbaceous perennials. Well-drained, but very moisture retentive soil during summer is essential to health, but otherwise they are relatively easy to grow, except in the coldest gardens where their South African 'roots' may let them down! Spring planting is important in such areas and mulching with bracken can help protect over-wintering corms. Most are garden hybrids. The oldest of all, tough, spreading 'montbretia' or *C.* × *crocosmiiflora* (40-60cm/16in-2ft) is naturalised widely in the mild west country climate and, since it tolerates even dry shade, is very useful for informal shrub or wild garden plantings. More refined plants for herbaceous borders include the superb flame red 'Lucifer' (1m/3¼ft); orange 'Emily McKenzie' (50-60cm/20in-2ft); bicoloured yellow and orange 'Jackanapes' (50-60cm/20in-2ft); lemon-yellow 'Citronella' (40-60cm/16in-2ft); and the lovely bronze foliage and yellow flowers of slightly frost-sensitive 'Solfaterre' (40-50cm/16-20in).

*Dierama* (Iridaceae) See page 79 (Mount Stewart)

*Eucomis* (Hyacinthaceae/Liliaceae). 'Pineapple Flower'. Eastern Cape of South Africa, Natal. Late summer. Spikes of fascinating, green, cream and yellow, starry flowers late in the season, crowned with small, leafy bracts and basal rosettes of glossy sometimes beautifully marked leaves. These are a must for the bulb enthusiast with a place at the base of a sunny, sheltered west or south-facing wall and the time to ensure that the soil does not dry out during summer. *E. bicolor* (30-40cm/12-16in) Purple-blotched stems, wavy-margined leaves and pale green flowers outlined in purple. *E. comosa* (to 60cm/2ft) Purple-spotted and striped stems and pale green, pinkish or purplish flowers with a

dark, central eye. *E. pallidiflora* (45-75cm/18-30in) Greenish-white flowers and long green wavy-edged leaves.

*Galtonia* (Hyacinthaceae/Liliaceae) See page 69 (Barrington Court)

*Gladiolus* (Iridaceae) South Africa, Mediterranean. The vast majority of the large-flowered hybrids, which are grown almost like bedding plants, with the frost-sensitive corms planted out each spring for cut flowers, are not included in this book. Many of the Head Gardeners do, however, cultivate the smaller, more graceful flowers of the 'Butterfly', 'Primulinus' and 'Nanus' groups. See page 69 (Barrington Court). *G. communis* subsp. *byzantinus* (60-90cm/2-3ft) Mediterranean. This is the hardiest gladiolus for British gardens with corms which may be planted in autumn. Graceful spikes of small, magenta-pink flowers in early summer build up to clumps on most soils, when given a sunny position.

*Lilium* (Liliaceae) Within this huge group of bulbs, there should be a lily for every garden. The bulbs are best planted as soon as received in early winter or spring, since they should not be allowed to dry out completely. Most lilies will grow on neutral to alkaline soil, but if your soil is particularly limy, then *L. candidum*, *L. chalcedonicum*, *L. pardalinum*, *L. henryi* and *L. pomponium* are good choices. Lilies which either tolerate or actively enjoy acid conditions include *L. martagon*, *L. hansonii*, *L. bulbiferum*, *L. henryi*, *L. davidii*, many of the Asiatic hybrids, *L. auratum*, *L. speciosum* and *L. pyrenaicum*. Poor soil drainage is perhaps the most frequent factor in failure with lilies. If your soil is very wet during winter dormancy, try planting individual bulbs onto small raised mounds of soil mixed with sharp sand, or consider growing in raised beds and containers. See pages 65, 73 and 46 (Barrington Court, Mount Stewart, Knightshayes). In addition to those suggested in the text, the following species and hybrids are excellent choices.

**Asiatic Hybrids** Derived from complex breeding programmes and generally very fine, easy to please garden plants. In addition to those given by Nigel Marshall at Mount Stewart, try 'Citronella' (1·2-1·5m/3¾-5ft) turk's cap, yellow, spotted brown; 'Connecticut King' (1m/3¼ft) upward-facing, orange; 'Corsage' (1·2m/3¾ft) outward-facing, creamy yellow and pink; 'Sterling Star' (1-1·2m/3¼-3¾ft) upward-facing, white with dark spots. *L. auratum* 'Golden-rayed lily' of Japan. 1-2m (3¼-6½ft). Five to ten fragrant, saucer-shaped, white flowers spotted crimson, with a yellow band along the centre of each petal. Must have lime-free soil.

**Bellingham hybrids** Part of a larger group of

American hybrids with turk's cap flowers, they are yellow to orangey-red, spotted darker red. Prefer very moist soil.

*L. bulbiferum* 1–1·5 m (3¼–5 ft) Cup-shaped, upright, reddish-orange flowers, spotted dark within. *L. b.* var. *croceum* produces stem bulbils.

*L. chalcedonicum* 1–1·2 m (3¼–4 ft) Brilliant red turk's cap flowers. Demands a sunny position. Apricot-coloured *L. × testaceum* is an old hybrid between this and *L. candidum*.

*L. hansonii* 1–1·5 m (3¼–5 ft) Orange-yellow, brown-spotted, turk's cap flowers. *L. × marhan* is a good hybrid between this and *L. martagon* with rich orange turk's cap flowers, spotted brown.

*L. henryi* To 2·5 m (8¼ ft). Ten to twenty large, orange turk's cap flowers. Very strong, easy to grow.

*L. pyrenaicum* 60–100 cm (2–3¼ ft) Greenish-yellow, turk's cap flower, streaked black at the centre. Var. *rubrum* is pure red. Easy to grow and, like *L. martagon*, naturalises well in grass. *L. pomponium* 30–90 cm (1–3 ft). Brilliant scarlet turk's cap flowers. Requires a warm position.

*Nomocharis* (Liliaceae) China. To 1 m (3¼ ft). Mid-summer. These lily relatives have elegant, saucer-shaped flowers, often with fringed edges and a beautiful pattern of darker speckles. Like lilies, their bulbs are best when not allowed to dry out and should be planted in autumn or early winter. They demand a moist, cool climate and, like rhododendrons, do best on free-draining, but moisture-retentive, acid soils. *N. aperta* has pale pink flowers with darker blotches and a purple eye. *N. mairei* has white flowers with reddish purple blotches over the petals and fringed outer petals.

*Tigridia pavonia* (Iridaceae) Mexico. 30–45 cm (12–18 in). Useful for adding a splash of colour where needed in the summer garden, although not frost-hardy. The short-lived iris-like flowers are very showy, in orange-red, yellow, white, reddish-purple and pink, often with beautiful contrasting markings. Tolerating temperatures down to about –8°C (18°F), they can be started off in spring protected in pots in cold frames, planted out then lifted in autumn after flowering.

*Watsonia* (Iridaceae) See page 77 (Mount Stewart)

## Autumn

**Autumn-flowering bulbs begin to grow after their dry summer dormancy, with the arrival of autumn rains. Unlike spring-flowering bulbs however, they produce their flowers immediately, although leaf production may be delayed (as in colchicum) until spring. Plant dormant bulbs or corms as soon as purchased in late spring or summer at twice the depth of the bulb unless otherwise stated.**

*Amaryllis belladonna* (Amaryllidaceae) See page 85 (Felbrigg Hall)

*Colchicum* (Colchicaceae/Liliaceae) See page 85 (Felbrigg Hall)

*Crocus speciosus* (Iridaceae) Autumn crocus. Greece, West Asia. 5–10 cm (2–4 in). Early autumn. There are a surprising number of crocus which flower in autumn, but this lilac-blue and deep violet veined species with beautiful orange stigmas is the most robust and will seed itself when established. Also available in white 'Albus' and deep blue, 'Conqueror'. Leaves appear after the flowers. For warm positions in shrub borders where the flowers will open to the sun and for naturalising in grass. Mowing regimes similar to that for colchicum.

*Cyclamen hederifolium* (Primulaceae) See pages 52 and 24 (Killerton, Nymans)

*Nerine bowdenii* (Amaryllidaceae) See page 24 (Nymans)

*Sternbergia lutea* (Amaryllidaceae) Mediterranean. 15 cm (6 in) Early autumn. Resembling large, yellow, goblet-shaped crocuses, their fleshy strap-shaped leaves, appearing with the flowers, betray their relationship with the daffodils. Require a warm position and will resent the overhanging foliage of neighbours which can reduce the 'baking' necessary to form flowers during summer dormancy. May be lifted and divided 'in the green' in late spring.

*Zephyranthes candida* (Amaryllidaceae) Rain Lily. Argentina, Uruguay. 15–20 cm (6–8 in) Early autumn. With large, white, upturned, crocus-like flowers at the same time as the rush-like leaves, this is the only frost-hardy species. Same treatment and conditions as for *Sternbergia*.

# Addresses

**Anglesey Abbey**
Lode, Cambridge CB5 9EJ

**Barrington Court**
Barrington, near Illminster, Somerset TA19 0NQ

**Erddig**
near Wrexham, Wales LL13 0YT

**Felbrigg Hall**
Felbrigg, Norwich, Norfolk NR11 8PR

**Killerton**
Broadclyst, Exeter, Devon EX5 3LE

**Knightshayes Court**
Bolham, Tiverton, Devon EX16 7RQ

**Mount Stewart**
Newtownards, Co. Down BT22 2AD

**Nymans**
Handcross, near Haywards Heath, West Sussex RH17 6EB

**Sissinghurst Castle**
Sissinghurst, near Cranbrook, Kent TN17 2AB

**Trelissick**
Feock, near Truro, Cornwall TR3 6QL

# Index